Bees on a Bicycle

Bees on a Bicycle

Finding Heart and Home in Small and Significant Ways

BY CATH SHAW TRUELOVE

Un-Settling Books
Boulder, Colorado USA

Cover Design: Karen Culp Photography + Design

Cover Art and Photography: Matt Lively

Typographer: Sally Wright Day

Editing: Maggie McReynolds

Author's Photo: Karen Culp Photography + Design

Interior photos courtesy of the Shaw and Truelove families unless otherwise noted.

ISBN: 978-1-7336371-0-7

For Mom, whose laughter and love of life guide me

Table of Contents

Chapter One: Tried Everything. 5

Chapter Two: Good Ol' Grief. 23

Chapter Three: False Starts; New Starts 47

Chapter Four: The Stuff of Life. 61

Chapter Five: Community for Better or Worse 77

Chapter Six: Learning to Listen 87

Chapter Seven: Bees' Beginnings, Our Beginnings. 101

Chapter Eight: Bees Blooms 127

Chapter Nine: Finding Beauty in Small 143

Conclusion: What's Next? 161

In Gratitude 163

About the Author. 167

Join the Bees Community! 169

    Continued conversations 169

    A special gift for our readers 169

Staying in touch 171

Readers' Guide 173

    Activities 173

    Questions 175

X *BEES ON A BICYCLE*

Introduction

Like those of approximately 50 percent of our population, my first marriage ended in divorce. I worked with my ex, and it made sense that he carry along with the business as the creative lead, so I was out of a job too. It was 2009. A lot of people were out of a job. I no longer had the company car, so I rode the bus. I applied for one, then tens, then hundreds of jobs—and waited for my life to start over. I was desperately sad, in a pivotal part of my life, and fumbling badly. Gossip swirled around me about the choices I was making. I admit, a few were a bit racy. Then, for good measure, things got worse. I lost my family. I got way over my head in a poor job choice. It was a big mess.

Fast forward a few years. Now, I have a rather odd sentence come out of my mouth from time to time: "I own most of the block from 19th to 20th on Market Street." I own a different business—a garden center called Bees on a Bicycle. I traded in my three-inch heels, camel-colored, fully-lined pants, and black turtlenecks for a pair of foamy sandals, sun-protective shirts, and a big hat.

In between was a topsy-turvy of adventure and heart-ache. I learned three major things:

1. **You can do so much more—with less.** I found purpose in the small, embraced minimalism, and made peace with losing life as I knew it.

2. **You are not in control.** If you want things to flow and go well, you had better give up, come out of your head, and say yes to what is possible. While you're at it, stop thinking you know what is going to happen next, and planning or predicting of any kind.

3. **If you plan to have others join you, get your act together**—both in your head and in your house. Stuff of all kinds simply gets in the way!

During all of this, Facebook posts were my creative outlet. I got messages that I was inspiring and that people found wisdom in my words. I, in turn, was inspired by the *Washington Post's* weekly series, "Life Is Short: Autobiography as Haiku," and modeled many of my posts on that style. I used it as a tool to hone my writing skills. People noticed and encouraged me. Meanwhile, I delayed writing anything lengthy because I didn't want people to have to wade through all my crap. Everyone has crap. Why should you read mine? Then Bees (my shorthand name for Bees on a Bicycle) happened. Life took a turn, and a book emerged.

In this book, I share bits of wisdom I gained along the way over the past few years. I went through hell to get them, and I hope that by reading them you can skip the hell part. The wisdom isn't rocket science or all new stuff either. What I offer here are reminders from my perspective on what makes life easier. For someone who tends toward sensitivities and a bit of...ahem...drama, I am all for life lessons making things easier!

Life isn't life if it doesn't change. Sometimes life deals out change in small doses. In my case, and probably yours too, change came in massive, non-bite-sized chunks. While drinking from this firehose, I was flummoxed and made mistakes. I was embarrassed, sad, and, frankly, pitiful at times. The reason I wrote it all down here is to make you smile, consider options, and dream. It is one thing to be called inspirational (I have been), but another to write to inspire. That is what I aim to do here: inspire. I want you to seek solace in my words and find a way for yourself too. Together, we can do hard things and big things. As Mom used to say, "We can move mountains!"

CHAPTER ONE:

Tried Everything

Do what you can, with what you have, where you are.

—Theodore Roosevelt

My career in trying everything started early in life.

In second grade, to prepare for parents' night, we were assigned a small essay: what we wanted to be when we grew up. I had no idea. Classmates wrote what they wanted to be; I wrote what I did *not* want to be—a doctor—and left everything else open to possibility. Dad thought that was fantastic and celebrated my creative approach. He put my inch-tall words in a frame and kept it on his desk for the rest of his life.

In high school, I would be preppy on a Tuesday, an edgy rock-and-roller on a Wednesday, and a forlorn innocent on Thursday. God knows what I was the other days.

Did you try that? Not all of us know who we are at that age, or have a great sense of self. I was the opposite of my friend Deborah at that time. She knew what she was and grew into that fully as an adult—a powerful Washington DC lawyer in an impressive house with a manicured lawn. Some of us lead linear lives and others, like me, take the scenic route.

From eighth grade through high school graduation, I went to four schools in five years. My parents were divorced and in new relationships, but were strict with me and prescriptive of my behavior. Perhaps this was because, for weeks and sometimes months, no one really kept tabs on me. As a result and like many kids, for me it was about getting through each day without making some sort of horrible mistake and embarrassing myself.

My dad's work had us moving often. Constantly being the new kid in town was a lot of work. I was busy keeping up with a continually rotating set of school halls, classmates, new towns, and cultures, often unsuccessfully. (I showed up at one new school in my Molly Hatchet concert t-shirt only to find myself surrounded by girls in silk dresses with pumps dyed to match.) College planning, college campus visits, and career goal-setting were not top of mind for me or my parents. We were too busy sorting out the current, continually shifting situation. So when it came time for college study, I simply chose the same major my dad chose years before and sent off my form to the state university.

Once at college, I had a garden-variety assortment of jobs to keep me in school, including photographer, library clerk, office assistant, and artist and runway model, among other weird pursuits. I was tall, dreadfully thin, red-haired, and, in the case of being an artist model, not pregnant, which is how I ended up replacing someone who was. I got very good at finding creative work that filled in the gaps between student aid, work-study programs, and grants. I hid my car at my boyfriend's house, safely away from the repo man, faithfully making every other payment and frustrating the bank to no end. I made it work somehow and wasn't above accepting a date when I was hungry or bored. I survived. As an interior design major, I did it somewhat glamorously too.

After college, the parade of pursuits continued. I was an interior designer, an association manager, and a school teacher for grades 2 and 5 and middle school math. After that, I owned the aforementioned branding agency for 13 years with my ex. Somewhere in there, I formed a small gardening company called The Garden of Urban to make ends meet while I got my master's degree in education.

With my marriage over and my branding business no longer mine, I sat down with this pile of disparate experiences. I was demoralized by my impending divorce and had lost touch with my identity during my agency-owning period—13 years was an amazingly long time for me to do just one thing. I was proud of what we had accomplished and had found a home in that role—but not a happy one.

Just writing a resume was a challenge, never mind finding work. My professional journey certainly wasn't the HR-preferred "progressively comprehensive and challenging" set of jobs with appropriate titles and salaries. I found myself among a not-young, not-old, in-between age of "what is this that I'm doing?" and "oh, hell, I have no idea" group of people in the same boat. For me, it was really scary. I took turns being excited about possibilities and then sitting down and crying because clearly no one on Earth would ever want to work with someone like me ever again. It was all just really confusing, mucky, and horrible.

I had lots of company. People who had been clients of our agency and owners of multimillion-dollar businesses were also looking for new work. Networking events were filled with folks out of a job for the first time in years, if not decades. A local mega-church formed a ministry to help thousands of us, broken into groups of 100 to make it easier all around. It was 2009. The housing crisis was in full swing, and it was an unsure time for many. All of us out of work and looking for our next opportunity.

The recession eventually ended. What endured, though, was the profound lack of confidence that we suffered if we were unemployed during that time. The bubble had burst. Many of us were left wondering what had happened and what was next. Also, for some of us, being at what some term "mid-career" was challenging as well. Post-recession, budget-conscious job ads asked for recent graduates primarily.

A deep sense of failure weighed heavily on me. From time to time, I'd also feel lost and aimless, for good measure. Social media fed this. Friends' advice, though helpful, held conflicting messages. Some wanted me to try something new, while others encouraged me to continue in the same vein, advancing as a communications professional. Dating advice also had many different angles and beliefs.

As a newly divorced woman, I was seeing a few guys and vividly experimenting in ways I hadn't been able to while married. It wasn't pretty and was probably embarrassing to people who knew me. Mercifully, I had the forethought not to share my adventures on Facebook, but most involved goodly sums of booze, parties, sex, and late nights. One night, I found myself in the middle of a golf course with my date tearing my clothes and wanting his way with me. Luckily, I was less drunk than he was, and a swift kick sent him reeling. I channeled my modelling days in heels and ran away like I'd been doing marathons in stilettos for years. That sobered me from my forays for a while, and I got more earnest about my job search. I was being unsafe and was damn lucky to be in one piece.

During this adventuresome period, lots of folks distanced themselves from me, and rightly so. I found myself with few friends, desperately lonely, unemployed, and divorced. It may have been my imagination, but it seemed like my neighbors would pretend to study a hangnail or a curb needing repair if they saw me out walking. Other neighbors were concerned and listened to my troubles. It was a hard time, and not everyone was prepared to handle what I was going through. One day, I found myself walking home from the park in our neighborhood. On one side of the street was my former home, complete with the gardens I had tended lovingly for years. On the other side was a rocking party of people I knew, visible through the picture windows. As an uninvited former friend, I walked alone up the street in tears.

Finally, I found something that worked. It was one of those pivotal, simple things that just happens. For me, this happened in my late forties. If you are lucky, it happens a lot earlier. What happened was that I took time to know myself. I took time to sort out what I liked, who I liked, and what represented me as a person, a friend, a mate, a coworker. Shakespeare's " to thine own self be true . . . " rang in my ears. I created an opportunity to make choices about myself that would carry me forward more consistently and, hopefully, successfully.

I realized that, much like those days in high school when I didn't know what outfit represented me, I didn't know on the inside what represented me either. I didn't know myself. If I didn't know myself, how on Earth would I select a profession or be of service to others? How would I know which friends were right for me? How would I even know what shirt to wear or what kind of food I liked? Never mind dating. No wonder that was a disaster. I had work to do.

Defining a sense of self can be fun and involve new clothes. It can also feel like being incredibly lost. I tended towards the latter. It isn't like you sit down and say, "Oh, this is me. From now on, I am doing things this way." Instead, it is a quiet noticing. It is taking note, making a stand for yourself, and saying no. When the time is right, it is also saying yes.

I might have had an easier time socially if I'd mastered this concept of knowing myself. The people I had considered my friends at one time, I realized, were a combination of neighbors, professional contacts, and drinking buddies. When it was time to clean out the house my ex and I owned, including the contents from our 1,500-square-foot studio space, I learned who my friends were. I remember driving back to my former home on moving day and seeing Jayne waiting there for me, leaning on her car. "Do you need someone to help you pack up your kitchen?" she asked. With a lump in my throat, I admitted I did, and much more. I made my first, dear, lifelong, first-tier, inner circle, at-my-deathbed friend that day. I learned something about myself: I wanted friends who showed up. I wanted folks who were there for me during thick and thin, and weren't too busy or embarrassed to be seen with me as I bumbled through divorce. I wanted Jayne, and she wanted me.

One can wish that, professionally, we can work out things more definitively. NOT. The human resource departments, resumes, job availability web sites, and all else wouldn't exist if it were all tidy and "just so." Life and our identities are messy, constantly changing and evolving. Meanwhile, companies change because of leadership, economic factors, market trends, and a whole slew of other elements. So, that said, it is uber-important to know thyself when entering the work force.

As someone new to the "know yourself" track, complete self-awareness wasn't yet possible. Becoming fully formed into a sense of self was my work in progress! I knew some aspects of what I was about, but had no idea when it came time to work and making a living. This became more and more of an issue as my unemployment checks didn't cover...much. I got really creative at selling things I owned (more on that later). During this time, I melted down random earrings without a match and necklaces I got as birthday gifts in high school. It amounted to hundreds of dollars and paid for groceries for months while I interviewed and hoped. I was one of three top candidates 19 times. Once I was offered a job, but before the start date, the leadership changed, and the job disappeared. It was like chasing my tail—all for jobs I frankly didn't want.

Much of the incentive to find myself came from Graham, a man I had begun dating. He was generous and kind and wanted to truly know me. He observed that I didn't know myself very well, and as a result presented somewhat of a mystery to him as a mate. After years of being told what I wanted by my mom and the men in my past relationships, I wasn't surprised. But here I was, in my 40s, and I wasn't going to hang the responsibility for this inspired self-discovery lesson on other people.

Graham came with a whopper of a last name—Truelove. He was tall, had a million-dollar smile, knew how to make a girl swoon (at least me), and was an amazing cook. He was the father of two, Henry and Julia, and they came first in his heart and life. He had his priorities straight, for sure. A trained mathematician, he was amazingly smart—a huge attractor for me. We shared a history of volunteer service, agreed on major political issues, loved modern architecture, and swam together at our community pool. He enjoyed spending time with me at the house

I was renting, and was well-liked by friends who knew us both. We loved cooking together, doing puzzles, and making fires. We eventually got a community garden plot together and grew vegetables and roses. He liked holding my hand and was downright eloquent about telling me what was in his heart. In a way, Graham was a bit of a Renaissance man who read classic literature, but repaired things too.

Early in our relationship, we met in a secluded spot in the pouring rain. We sat in our raincoats for hours, shivering and sharing stories, getting to know each other. I shook also from excitement but primarily from cold. Graham was a great listener and really wanted to know about me. In a way, he was proper in his questioning and very charming.

I kissed him and he kissed me back. He backed me up against a wall and really went for it. Rain be darned, we wanted to kiss each other that day. I said, "You seem like the kind of guy who could make love to a woman for hours."

"Days," he replied.

I about fell over. I didn't know what swooning was prior to that moment, but swear I learned what swooning was right then and there. Oh my goodness. This was powerful stuff.

And he was a neighbor in a very tight-knit community. This could be complicated. He sat on the pool board, and lots of neighbors knew him. My ex and I were also well-known. We had done communications and design work for both the pool and the neighborhood. Through our dogs and various neighborhood events, we knew lots of people too.

Our neighborhood had an online email discussion group, and we all were active on it. The group had rules, and one was not to discuss politics. The email list was for neighborhood issues only. Though the rules stated otherwise, my ex and Graham's brother and his dad got into a political battle, with emails back and forth and copied to hundreds of others on the list. When I was still married, we considered the Trueloves a bad family and not to be discussed. We were kind of like the Sharks and the Jets in *West Side Story*. Graham was one of THEM.

I decided to tell my ex first before anyone else knew who I was seeing. My ex and I were separated, I was living outside our home, and we had agreed that dating was permitted. We were still working together in our business at that point so I saw my ex almost every weekday.

"Hi. I need to tell you about someone I am seeing," I said.

"Who?"

"Graham Truelove," I replied.

"Well, make me eat a shit sandwich," he said.

The opposing family had been revealed, and I was dating one of them. Then, for good measure, I moved in with him.

Though I had moved out of my home with my ex months before, the transition with his kids and those around us in the neighborhood, in retrospect, was incredibly fast. I knew this (but ignored advice) because people told me as much. "Date for a few years, then see where

Cath and Graham laughing together

it goes" was the most typical advice, among other per-
spectives offered. I didn't want to take advice. I wanted to
move right away, and did. Graham was a great guy, and I
wanted to spend as much time as I could with him.

In our neighborhood, there were so many places affil-
iated with the two of us that Graham and I had to name
them to keep them straight. The house I lived in when I
was separated became "the little house." The one my ex
and I owned became "the big house." Graham's house,
a block from the little house was eventually called "our
house." Graham's mom lived a few doors down, and her
house was called "Grannie's house." His kids lived with
his ex a few blocks away, and that was "Susan's house."
And his brother was also in the same neighborhood so we
called his house "Paul's house." Whew! We joked that the

Trueloves needed a whole page in the community phone directory! Eventually I'd move from the big house to the little house, back to the big house to sell it, then to Graham's (eventually our) house.

With so many family households nearby and with his volunteering for years in the community pool, I was dating someone well-known, but intensely private and quiet. Other single women asked me how I found him. My response was usually, "I found him hidden under a rock." He had been divorced for ten years, but had been focused on being a good dad since. The ultimate motivation to move in together was because it made sense financially, and, well, we had great chemistry together. There was just something about that guy that made me swoon. Since I'd sold my share of the business to my ex, I was unemployed. Graham was also unemployed at that time, and I could help him make ends meet rather than renting elsewhere. Two unemployed people in one house was a challenge. We were as poor as church mice, but happy and in love.

Once we lived together, Graham noticed my spending habits. As a team in the same house, it made sense to talk about it. I remember him asking me about shopping at thrift stores. I said, "Yes, I go to Loehmann's all the time." For those of you who don't know about the now-defunct Loehmann's, it was a shop that had a great back room with all the top designers. It was *not* a thrift store, by any means. When Graham picked himself up off the floor from laughing, he took me to a large thrift store. I was embarrassed and worried that someone would see me. It took a while, but eventually I became an enthusiastic thrift store shopper and marveled at what was there for the price. If you knew textiles and color theory like I did from my interior design education, shopping this way was really fun.

A neighbor, Lise, also shopped at this same thrift store. We began comparing notes and sharing victories. Her dog Charlie got along with my dog Bea (a very rare thing for Bea), and we'd go for long walks and have amazing conversations. She understood my embarrassment and my efforts at stretching financially. She supported me in ways I hadn't been supported before—by listening, sometimes for hours, in conversations that stretched over weeks of those walks with our dogs. I added her, alongside Jayne, to my list of gals who would become lifelong friends. Like Jayne before her, Lise showed up two years later when we were packing up Graham's house after it sold. What is it about packing kitchen stuff? Clearly, for me, it is a ticket to lifelong friendship! In all seriousness though, the key element was showing up—being present. This was the one, most important thing I learned with my new dear friends that I will put into action the rest of my life. The other was open and honest communication.

For extra points in my thriftiness education, Graham took me dumpster diving. Again, I was afraid someone would see me, and I would be mortally embarrassed. We needed plants for the house, and soon we had several six-foot beauties that had been tossed out behind an office building, complete with great containers.

The two of us set a budget of around $30 a week for

groceries and ate like kings. Graham is one of the thrift-
iest people I've ever met. He came home recently and
said, "Look at these sunglasses I found on the side of the
road!" He gave them a good washing and has worn them
for months. Our barbeque has similar origins. We don't
steal, but the list of things we don't pay for, or buy in smart
ways, is a long one.

In short, I learned that not spending money could do
a soul good. In a land of people who soothe their losses or
lack with a bowl of ice cream, a new pair of shoes, or even
a new car, this was an opposite tack I found refreshing.
I learned to find joy in simplicity and frugality. A walk
in the woods, a cup of tea, or raking leaves together took
on new meaning. This was a big step for me—I'm my
Mom's daughter, and she had a flair for purchasing. It was
a whole new world, yet dovetailed with my love for architectural simplicity and minimalism. I found myself studying moments, shared experiences, and my surroundings
in new way.

For example, one day I looked at our dining room
table. I saw the light cast upon it, the dishes left from breakfast, the location next to a window where deer walked by.
Memories and moments circled that table, even though
I'd only lived with it for weeks. I sat there quietly noticing,
observing. This was a big change from my former professional role, heading off to $40 networking breakfasts.
Instead, that table freed me to imagine. It gave comfort
and support, rather than clutter and overwhelm. I found
a whole new world in chosen, cherished objects. Such
power and grace I learned and allowed myself as I sat

there at that table with my tea.

Unlike me back in those days, Graham knew himself to the core. When something didn't sit well with him, you immediately knew or he communicated it in his quiet, peaceful way. It was just maddening if you were lost and trying to find yourself like I was! We'd have great discussions on the topic at hand, after which I felt like an idiot because I didn't know myself well enough to fully state my opinions. It was a confusing time for me.

During this time, probably on one of the days I felt confused and not very confident, Graham decided to find a job. I walked him to the front yard, took a professional headshot, and redid his LinkedIn profile. He submitted a few resumes. A few days later, he had an interview and they offered him the job—two hours' drive away. He put them on hold to talk to me. "I'd better take this," he said. I agreed. Our little household couldn't live on great sexual chemistry, $30 grocery runs, and dumpster fun forever. He also had mounting obligations for his children, their advanced education to consider, and house payments. Ah, reality. Ah, work. New beginnings.

With Graham employed, that left me to look at my work life more closely. I realized that one thing I was good at and that suited me was sales. It was my primary role in our branding agency. When I was doing interior design in an entry-level position, I was told that I "had the gift of gab" and could make a pitch like the partners. I loved presenting ideas and seeing if people were ready.

As a result of this revelation, I got involved in a multi-level marketing business, selling thousands of dollars of essential oils a month. It was fun and I met people but it was a lot of alone time and cheerleading, and that wasn't me. Add that to my resume. I also tried business consulting; I worked with clients to ease their way into entrepreneurial life, create systems, and market effectively. If you value working alone and aren't lonely like I was, that is the job for you! Eventually I moved on from that too, but must say that from time to time I still do it and enjoy it tremendously.

While Graham worked two hours south in Richmond, I continued my job search for full-time employment. Having him gone during the week was an unexpected blessing—I badly needed the time to sort out more about my identity. On the weekends, Graham would come home to see his son Henry (daughter Julia was away in college), his house, and me. We commuted like that for over four years.

After 14 months of searching and interviewing, I got a job! I was hired as a technical writer for a semi-governmental agency in the mortgage arena. I'd be managing a team of three people and overseeing online as well as published writing. It would be my first corporate job since 1995. Coming as I was from a business with a handful of employees to a campus with several buildings and a corporate cafeteria, it was a big adjustment.

It was a bit touch-and-go before starting, though. In true DC style, there was a background check where they confirmed my previous salary. As a business owner, my salary had fluctuated quarterly, depending on sales, for over a decade. My hiring status was referred to the company's legal department, and I found myself trying to explain entrepreneurial salary fluctuations in a way that didn't reduce my chances of landing the job. I wrote a small essay explaining common fluctuations in entrepreneurial compensation. The explanation was accepted, and off I went—but I needed wheels to get to work.

For approximately two years before I got a job, I was unable to afford a car. Along with my thrift store and dumpster identity challenges, riding the bus was a new thing for this BMW and Volvo S Series girl. In short, riding the bus was amazing—but didn't transport me to my new job easily. I met great people and had amazing conversations. I learned new things. I stretched in new ways I never thought I would. I will say that it took amazing amounts of time too. But being unemployed, I had lots of time to spare.

So to get me ready for a new job, my mom, who did more mothering of me in my 40s than all the other times in my life, gave me a small loan. I purchased a Hyundai hatchback that I still drive. I drove it proudly to my new job and parked it among the Mercedes, Audis, and other luxury vehicles of my coworkers. I was proud I owned a car at all.

CHAPTER TWO:

Good Ol' Grief

Grief can be the garden for compassion.
If you keep your heart open through everything,
your heart can become your greatest ally
in your life's search for love and wisdom.

—Rumi

I believe we all have a "Spidey-sense" at birth, but it mostly gets socialized out of us. Mine is pretty refined and comes in handy when working with animals or plants. I get messages from time to time about upcoming events. I have known in advance that people were getting a job, going to date someone significant, or move away suddenly. Mostly I keep this news to myself and let life unfold. Society doesn't act on extrasensory messages generally, and I respect that. Sometimes people have a strong recollection of present events having occurred already, and we call that déjà vu. Where I am different is pre-cognition—sensing things in advance.

When it came to what I sensed, I was particularly accurate with events having to do with my mom. Maybe this was because she was the last remaining member of my immediate family. I'm not really sure why.

My dad had died a few years before my divorce. Mom, like my dad, was an only child, and so was I. As an only child of two only children, that meant that I had no siblings, cousins, aunts, or uncles. My immediate family, in its entirety, was Mom.

Mom and I had a close relationship, but a hard one. She had a strict upbringing and raised me with very tight reins. Then, with a confusing teeter-totter effect, she'd leave me alone to my own devices. While I was in high school, for example, I lived for weeks at a time alone while Mom and her second husband traveled the world.

While I was married to my ex, Mom and I traveled together too. This was the highlight of our relationship together for many years.

In this relationship between Mom and me, I too was no saint. Like many of us, I can be hard on people, and boy, was I hard on my mom. I shut her out and didn't share much of my life with her. This all changed when I took the Landmark Forum, something I wish I'd done in my twenties. It was eye-opening, with life lessons I hadn't gotten through years of therapy, self-help books, and workshops.

Lessons or aha moments are called "distinctions" by Landmark Education, and are named for easy reference later for graduates. One distinction, in particular, is called "creating a new possibility." There is a certain format in which Landmark teaches you to do this, and I tried it one day with Mom. I talked with her about the possibility of a different kind of relationship with me, one of fun, adventure, and love. We sat together on the sofa and were about to eat dinner. It wasn't a formal thing or one that took a long time. It did carry a lot of weight, though, and we both listened to each other as I went through the steps. It was amazing how it worked. Landmark came up with that process after 50 years of evolution, beginning with EST in 1971, and it is profound. We both cried, agreed we wanted something better, and never looked back. Our lives together were forever changed.

Even before we had this particularly close bond, I told her what I sensed. I'm not a true psychic, but just feel things. It had one practical application: the phone. Before cell phones with country-wide coverage, we had to pay per long distance call. It got expensive! So for years, I used this sensitivity to my advantage. When she was about to call or I wanted to save money by having her call me, I'd just sit down and think about it—and the phone would ring. Everyone does that, right? I have superpowers, and so do you!

Four years before I began this new job, I had a premonition. Mom was heading to a funeral, and I had a premonition that there was danger there. I shared this with her and asked her not to go. She called the next day and said she would be attending, and off she went. We hadn't heard from her for ten days when the hospital called. She had been in intensive care with nine broken bones after being thrown from the vehicle on the way from the airport. She hadn't gotten her seatbelt on yet, and when the car spun around, she flew out the broken back window onto the median. It was a miracle she was alive.

The accident was in Colorado, and Mom was transported back to Arizona, where she'd lived since taking care of her dad there in the late 90s. I headed to her house to help. I looked at her on the sofa in her living room. "You look so broken," was all I could think (and said to her). She was a mess of broken bones, bruises, and massive amounts of pain. I didn't say "I told you so," but we both had an unspoken conversation about how I knew in advance that things would go this way. She didn't believe me, though, and overrode my recommendation. So there was her situation—it just was. That was not the time to lecture or judge. There were doctor's appointments, physical therapy, new glasses to buy, and a myriad of details to tend to. We glued Mom back together somehow, and years later when I got my new job, she was there in one piece on the other end of the phone.

I was a week or so into my new position when I got a call at work from one of Mom's doctors. It was a medical office where she had gotten a mammogram a few days before. They'd seen an issue with her heart on the films and needed to reach her immediately. I was listed as next of kin, and they called me when they couldn't find her. It was a Tuesday afternoon, and I sat down and thought. I wasn't really familiar with Mom's schedule then, because of my new job and the search for it that had occupied the previous 14 months. As a result, I had no idea where she was. Instead, I got quiet, and words came to me: "She's at church."

"On a Tuesday?" they asked.

"I don't know, but that's where she is," I said.

So I called the church, and the receptionist said, "Yeah, Sandy's sitting right here. Do you want to talk to her?"

I can't remember exactly what we organized next, but she was whisked away to the hospital and not allowed to drive. In short, via a mammogram of all things, they had discovered an aneurysm in the aortic arch of her heart. What we didn't know at that point was that the aneurysm was caused by the accident, four years before. Go get your mammograms, girls!

Meanwhile, I was in week two of my new job overseeing the technical writing of more than a hundred documents at once. It was a prominent six-figure position with hundreds of daily emails, meetings, presentations, a team to manage, and an enormous learning curve. Ironically, the architectural plans for the building we worked in were on the drafting boards at one of the two interior design jobs I had in the early 90s. It was like coming full circle.

As a new employee, I took calls privately to monitor Mom's progress pre-surgery and throughout the days of intensive care right after. "No sense having you come out here with all this staff here at the hospital and all my friends here every day," she said. We agreed that Graham and I would come take care of her when she returned home ten days after the surgery.

When we arrived, I slept in the hospital bed, and Mom preferred the hospital chair. Between my new responsibilities at work and what was going on with her, I was beyond exhausted. Mom was agitated and ready to get out the hospital. Graham was a rock. He took care of both of us.

Graham and I were caretakers for ten days at Mom's house and got things in working order. Her surgery included a thousand stitches in her heart, much follow up, and detailed healing protocols. I remember Mom wanting a shower badly. It had been weeks since a real dousing with water, and she was desperate. The only shower in her house was upstairs, and she was determined. Up we went with doctor approval. It took half an hour, but we did it. Good grief.

Once in the shower, she couldn't do anything. I was dressed and scrubbing and getting soaked. Finally, I took my clothes off and did a proper back scrubbing for her. We Shaw girls embraced our nudity that day. She sighed as the warm water fell down on her body. I was so honored to be standing there to witness this sweet relief.

Days later, we handed over caretaking responsibility to Mom's friend of 54 years, Diddy. Diddy was a nurse, so that was an added bonus. Mom was assigned to take five-minute walks, and had strapped on her sneakers to come say goodbye to us in the driveway.

Again, I had a strong intuition feeling. This time I didn't say anything. Instead, I just cupped her face in my hands and said, "I love you so much" and cried. I cried on the way to the airport. I cried on the plane. I was just overcome with dread.

She died suddenly two days later. The aneurysm was resolved by the surgery, but then she threw a clot and died. It happens in a percentage of heart surgeries. I was on the phone with Diddy, and she knocked on the bathroom door and found Mom. I heard Diddy trying to rouse her and waited on the other end of the phone in Virginia. Hours later, they confirmed what I already knew. Mom was gone—she died before hitting the floor. People from all aspects of her life were there that night for a pizza party —folks from her professional life, gals from the gym, fellow parishioners from her church. She certainly wasn't alone when she passed.

Sometimes, just when you think it can't get any worse, it does. Someone or several people die. It seems endless. Is your dog still alive? Your marriage? Family members dropping like flies? In my case, within two years, it was my business, my marriage, several of my friends, my home with my ex, and my Mom. The amount of loss made my head spin.

Before Mom, there was Beatrice, my dog. She was a fear biter. For four and a half years, she would gear up and run and bite someone randomly. Folks would try to pet her silky fur, and she would strain at the leash, bark, and snap aggressively. If done just right, meetings could go well, but never consistently. It got worse as I divorced. One day, she bit my inner thigh. Ouch. A neighbor who knew Bea said, "You need to do something about that dog," and I agreed. Graham had a small niece and nephews, and I wouldn't forgive myself if they were attacked. I consulted again with trainers and the rescue organization I was obligated to notify if I thought about giving her up.

"Is she always like this?" they asked after Bea tried to attack. "Does she sleep like the dead?" Evidently, this indicated exhaustion from extreme anxiety. "She is fearful, and it will only get worse and more dangerous for her and you and all who come in contact with her. Here are your options." I thought hard and cried, then I said goodbye to Bea.

By my choice, I lost my dog. My marriage had ended. I had sold the business I helped build. I sold my house. Now I had lost my mother. As an only child of two only children, Mom was the last of my immediate family. I was the last of the Shaws alive in our branch of the family, which I found to be tremendously sad.

I had a new job, but it certainly wasn't a cure-all. In fact, I quit that job after nine months.

I remember the two weeks between giving notice and leaving were like being a Catholic priest in confessional. One after another, coworkers confessed their distaste for working there and reasons why. "I wouldn't be here if not for my kids in [private] school," and "We moved recently, and I need to stay here because of the [larger/more expensive] house," and so on. Choices, including all those luxury cars parked near my Hyundai, necessitated ongoing work obligations. I listened and moved on as quickly as I could. I knew from my self-investigations that I was distinctly different from them and had a different path. Those moments with tea at our dining table were the beckoning of a better and simpler life for me. This choice came with risk—jobs were still hard to find in that economic climate. People coming to my makeshift confessional said I was brave and courageous, and admired my choice.

In that nine months I'd been working, using the thrifty skills Graham had taught me, I'd saved $60,000. I literally didn't know where to spend the money after living off of nearly nothing and riding the bus! I could survive for a long, long time on that. I wanted space to sit and think and grieve. I needed to find a good spot away from home and Graham to do this. He and I didn't take a break, per se, but at this juncture, it was important to live apart.

One of the things that I have consulted on and spoken about in speeches is the concept of flow. This is how flow works. You go exploring and like a really chic, historical, riverside town, in this case, Chestertown, Maryland. You return home to Northern Virginia and look at Craigslist. You find a listing for a 200-square-foot building on a cobblestone street two blocks from the river in the heart of the historic district for an insanely low price. You rent it the next day for five months. You go sit near the river and take deep breaths—lots of them. Chestertown, on the banks of the Chester River, had all the charm and good food I needed. It was full of history and adventure, and I needed diversion.

Flow. Go with the flow. Don't fight it. Do what works. These words rang in my head and guided me. We all call flow something along these lines. Football teams swear by it as they work together wordlessly to strategize seamlessly on the field. I love this concept. I embraced it and moved into what would now be called a tiny house. I washed my dishes in the bathroom sink and didn't have a stove, but I didn't care. There were mountains of peach ice cream to eat for breakfast and farmers' markets full of fresh tomatoes. I sat and grieved. I let go and practiced moving on.

Best of all, I entertained friends. It was amazing how people show up when you are in the flow. I loved this concept with business, but here I was putting it to use in a great life adventure. And adventure it was: rest came on an air mattress in this tiny, converted historical smokehouse. No worries. Many friends came and slept there on that air thing and ate tomatoes with me. It was simple, magical, and sweet. It was so needed.

One of my favorite activities while in Chestertown was to get on a road and drive until the road ended. At that part of Maryland near the Chesapeake, there were lots of peninsulas and water, so it is easy to find roads like that. Typically, I'd take a sandwich with me and have a little picnic by the water. Sometimes I'd swim, dodging sea nettles. I had a folding chair, and I'd pull it out of the car and read library books. I'd read really crazy romantic fiction from the public library. Some of the books were downright racy! I had such fun noting that tax dollars had bought such romance and frivolity for we library patrons! I was happy.

In between guests, I learned how best to be alone and live life fully. Mom's death had taught me that, and I did a masterful job at it that summer. I spent many hours enjoying life, breathing it in from a beach chair or a bar stool, sipping martinis. In the morning, I'd stroll the brick-lined streets to go to the local bakery and sleepily sip latte from a large mug. To entertain myself, I'd photograph gardens or birds. It was idyllic.

Sitting by the water was a great way to remember my mom and the times we had together. We found that we got along best when we travelled together. After healing from the accident, she celebrated and booked us a ten-day cruise to Alaska. She wasn't aware that I had a fear of ships after watching the *Poseidon Adventure* and *Titanic* numerous times. I powered on bravely, and we had a grand adventure together.

Mom and Cath in Alaska

When I turned 40, the destination became my choice. Mom was aghast when I chose Disney World over various tropical spots, but went along gamely. We rode all the smaller roller coasters, despite her declaration she wouldn't set foot on one. We spent afternoons at the water park with Mom attempting not to get her hair wet. She got hosed down by one of the ambassadors, which made that water park day a whole lot easier. The high point was dinner at The Artist Point in The Wilderness Lodge, after which a wooden Adirondack boat met us on the dock to shuttle us to the fireworks and meet Mickey Mouse. I may have been turning 40, but I was in heaven. After the festivities, the boat picked us up again and whisked us away. My memories of travelling with Mom were happy ones.

During this time in Chestertown, reflecting by the water, I also realized that living with someone was a concession! Boy, did I love living alone. As fabulous as Graham is, I find it a compromise to live with him or anyone else. You can't decide you want to get up and grill a cheese sandwich at 2 a.m. for fear of waking them, for example. Yes, there are many advantages to living as a couple, family, or whatever combination, but living and being alone can be a great luxury. If you haven't mastered it, I highly recommend it, particularly if you are still working on developing a sense of self like I was then.

A version of being alone, while together with someone, is asking for space. I've dated and been married most of my adult life, and I just added this request to my quiver of self-care skills. If you can't amass thousands of dollars and live near a river, just ask for space. Go do something by yourself that you love. It can be as simple as sitting on a park bench with a big thermos of tea. Be good to yourself, by yourself. It is sublime self-care 101.

Many of my friends and customers have family, work, church, and other obligations. They have a sense of responsibility, and there's nothing wrong with that. There comes a time, though, which I vividly realized there by the river, for sitting down and doing nothing. Kids get a time-out when all hell is breaking loose, so why can't we? We can. And we will, if we have the courage.

That summer in Chestertown was an exercise in stripping down to nothing. I lived in a 200-square-foot building and put all that I needed to survive into my Hyundai hatchback. There was no closet, so a few hooks held the dresses and shirts I chose to come with me. It taught me how truly few items we need to live comfortably. I got a profound sense of who I was by what I carefully selected to be in my home and who I invited to spend time with me. After losing my job (by my choice) in addition to all the other loss in my life, I was finding a further-refined and solid sense of self I enjoyed immensely.

After sitting by the Chester River for five months, I needed to stand back up. Oddball items from Mom's estate, and also Dad's, were piling up. I needed to sit at a desk, rather than avoiding one. There was work to be done. Among other things, I had received a $700 water bill from Mom's house, which was sitting empty with the toilet only getting flushed by a realtor every week or so. I read the bill closely without my glasses: 5,000 gallons. Seriously? I called the water company in Arizona. "No, no, honey, that's 50,000 gallons," she said. Oh. My. God. I hired contractors, who dug up the driveway and found the leak. Then we repaved. Then we dug it up again for another leak a few months later. I came back to reality quickly, and my $60,000 got spent more rapidly than I'd hoped. Thank God I sat down first to breathe in Chestertown!

Though my dad had died five years earlier, his estate was getting complicated at the same time I managed Mom's estate. Dad used to joke, "Wait until I'm gone. You'll be chasing after buildings all over the country and sorting things out for years!" And I did. Dad loved to drive around the Midwest, happen upon an auction for abandoned buildings for back taxes, and buy them for pennies on the dollar. At the time he made this revelation about me chasing around buildings, I said something along the lines of, "Yeah, yeah, Dad," and didn't believe him. Well, come to find out, Dad had registered his property management company at my address. Now that he was dead, I'd get calls about said buildings and back tax bills that he (and thus me as his heir) owed.

One building in Oklahoma was particularly worrisome. I looked it up in Google Maps and "walked" down the road to see its environs. It was a ghost town. I called the city it was in about the years of back taxes. "Uh. You don't want to tangle with that building, dear. It is infested with, like, 300 cats. It smells real bad," the clerk told me. After briefly (i.e., for an hour) considering starting an artist colony in this abandoned space, I filed paperwork to allow it to be sold for taxes. For me, estate work was a seemingly never-ending set of problems to solve. I'd worked on Dad's estate for five years and was about to dive into three years sorting out my mom's.

One of the wealthiest people I know once said, "Your

dad will make and lose more money than all of us sitting here around this table combined," and that is probably true. Dad was a successful civil engineer who managed complex construction projects in several continents. As his only child, I travelled along. I was born in Venezuela when he was managing a dam being built there. I learned to swim in Australia as he managed a railroad, iron ore plant, and development of a small city to support these enterprises. I traveled alone to him in Abu Dhabi at age 14. That venture involved an overnight stop in London where I stayed with his assistant, whom I'd never met.

Cath and her dad in Egypt
after the summer in Abu Dhabi

As he rose in stature, he bought real estate. When he went bankrupt the first time, just as I needed funds for college, he owned 23 houses and 17 condos. As a teen, I'd often accompany him as he selected a new place to buy.

I'd give advice on kitchens and neighborhoods I preferred. In addition to the houses, an 83-foot yacht was anchored in the island of Malta in the Mediterranean with a full-time skipper. Did he die with a penny to his name? No.

Smarts and retaining wealth are two different things. He definitely had smarts. When friends dared him to take the Mensa IQ test, Dad went in without any prep at all, scored in the 98th percentile, and was awarded a lifetime membership in the organization.

And then there's retaining wealth. Dad loved risk. His friend told me, "See that road? Your dad owns it. He drives so damn fast all the tickets paid for all that pavement." The futures market got hold of all his savings and his sense of what was possible. His brilliant mathematical mind thought he could figure out the future and gain from it. He gained substantially and lost far more. During this time of sorting Mom's estate, the Feds came after me, Dad's executor, for millions in taxes. I had to prove Dad's losses. It was relatively easy, but involved lists of phone calls, forms, and patience.

As I sorted out tax obligations for Dad, I recalled when I first got a sense that there was something amiss financially for him. When Dad dropped me off at college, my car got a flat and was illegally parked. We had just emptied out his car and mine of my earthly belongings, and they were sitting on the sidewalk. He looked at his watch and said, "I have an appointment and need to go. This is one of the many things you'll learn in college. Remember, not all the learning is done in class," and left. He was right, but I sure would have liked help from him sorting out the flat tire and all my belongings on the sidewalk.

Months before the college sidewalk incident, I was working at my pharmacy assistant job as a senior in high school. He met me at work and said, "I'm moving to Clear Lake," [two hours away] and drove off. I was left living in a condo with his second wife, whom he was divorcing. Mom was up the road in Dallas at the time and also didn't step up either. I did drugs. Go figure.

Cath in high school after her dad left

I began to understand my parents' priorities back in 7th grade when I got the lead for the dance recital. All the other parents were in attendance, eager to see their offspring perform. Mine went on vacation to Vancouver. As a fitting tribute, the recital piece I was in was a modern dance number illustrating our favorite color. I chose black.

One of the things that I was exposed to in Landmark Education is the concept of our parents doing the best they can. It isn't like they give birth and say, "Gosh, I'd like to be the worst parent ever!" As I managed their estates, I came to terms with this—too late to share this insight with them. Sure, I'd do something completely different as a parent. But they didn't. They did the best they could. What I didn't know on the sidewalk at college that day was that Dad was going bankrupt and scrambling. He probably left so he could find a way to pay for my education.

Instead, Dad prepared me for college by handing me

Cath and her parents before they divorced

a brown paper bag. Inside it was a potato smasher like you'd use to make mashed potatoes, a melon-ball maker, and a meat grinder. I, a new college coed, looked at him and wondered what to do with them. I lived in a dorm with a cafeteria that made over 20,000 meals a day. "You never know when you will need one of those," he said. I kept the melon-ball tool for years in hopes of party-girl greatness. Drunk people at parties in search of a bottle opener would look at it and pretend it was a telephone handset. It was a source of many laughs and eventually didn't make the cut in one of my many moves.

My dad managed multimillion-dollar projects—billions in today's numbers—and he taught me all that I know about management, office politics, and steering through corporate tangles. When we talked by phone, we'd scheme for hours about how to best navigate the personalities and policy. He was my sole advisor while employed by an association where I was in the right place at the right time. I was tapped to address an issue affecting architects nationwide: The Americans with Disability Act. As a result, I was selected to manage the first million-dollar project for the association where I worked at the time—at the ripe age of 25. Men twice my age wondered what had happened. I worked my tail off and kept my head down. When I admitted I needed help, eight people were hired to accommodate the workload that I had handled for months.

I know in my heart that Dad adored me. He just wasn't what I would call an A+ student in applying his adoration for practical parenting and upbringing of me, his daughter.

When he was buried, we didn't really bury him, we buried her. We never fully knew until he told me and my ex that *he* identified as *she* in 2002. When I was younger, I had hints that something was not "all Dad." For example, when I was a kid, I had a great dress that people often admired. I'd thank them and say, "My dad bought this for me," and people would look at me strangely. I thought everyone's dad had great taste in female clothing, but caught their cause for pause in conversation.

Transgender life was talked about less in 2002 than it is today, and I wasn't prepared, even though I was in my 30s at the time and had considered myself to be open to all sexual orientations. What was hard was reframing the whole picture of my dad and who he was in a single conversation, a moment. When he told us, I was sitting on a sofa and thought the springs had broken. I felt like I was falling in a hole; the effect of the information was so powerful. It was a massive shift in perception and understanding that rocked me. Looking back, I believe he told us because he knew that eventually we would be cleaning out his house when he died. When that time actually came, I found his closet filled with female clothing.

My dad died legally as Stephanie Williams. At least, that is what his driver's license read. He had a permission slip in his wallet from Veteran Affairs (VA), where he received medical care, and it allowed him to use the women's bathroom at the VA hospital. Dad was giving speeches on being transgender decades before it came to be discussed openly in schools and the workplace. And he did this *in the military*, and later in his career as a civil engineer managing large construction projects all over the globe. Can you imagine being in that predominantly all-male work environment and identifying as another sex entirely? What a balancing act! He built railroads, small cities to house workers, iron ore plants, pipelines, and dams. Dad was not your average gal.

Dad was more of a feminist than my mother. If he were alive today, he'd be right beside me, marching for female rights and equalities. He taught me about Gloria Steinem and books like *The Women's Room,* by Marilyn French. If my voice was too high-pitched, in his opinion, he would ask me to lower it. "You'll never get anything asking for what you want like that," he'd say. "Say it again." It was discouraging, but prepared me for years working with predominantly-male fields of web design and architecture in the 1980s–90s.

Dad was a Seabee, part of the US Navy construction force during the Korean War. He was a surveyor. I asked him what he surveyed, and he replied, "Guam."

"What do you mean? The airport or what?" I asked.

"No, the whole island," he replied. He and his team had surveyed the whole darn island!

As a result of his military standing, Dad not only got medical care from the VA, but he was qualified to be buried in Arlington National Cemetery outside Washington DC.

My parents' two estates collided the day after Mom died. I woke up and somehow knew that Arlington Cemetery, even though they had not been in touch for months about my dad's burial, was going to phone that day—and they did. They were finally ready to bury Dad (well, his ashes, anyway). I delayed them, since I now had to deal with burying my mom. But while you can delay the Army once, you cannot do so twice.

We buried Dad just weeks after Mom, five years after he died. Jayne went with me, and the two of us were the only two in attendance other than Army officials. Afterward we went to the Ritz Carlton and drank martinis, Mom's favorite drink, and one that I'd developed a taste for. A small memorial celebration, of sorts, for two dead parents.

To keep my sanity while managing these estates and the details involved in my divorce, I volunteered to foster a parade of dogs. I got to know dozens of fine, dedicated souls who cared for animals in need. I also met many, many fine animals who were great companions to me at this trying time in my life. I became one of those "crazy people" who asked if I could visit the home of potential adoptees of a pet I'd fostered. I learned why—it is one sure way to determine if someone wasn't hoarding animals. All in all, I fostered 13 dogs.

I also continued volunteering at the community pool where Graham sat on the board and managed the grounds. Before we began seeing each other, and prior to my separation, Graham had recruited me as a volunteer. He'd asked me to come see what I thought about the gardens at the pool. He'd cooked me an amazing dinner. It had been pouring rain, and we'd sat under a huge beach umbrella as Graham barbequed. Later, I was asked what he was like. "He is a lonely and sad man," I'd said. Later,

I learned that Graham had described me at that time as bossy and opinionated. Needless to say, our sexual chemistry hadn't surfaced.

Our community pool had eight or ten garden beds, the largest of which was over 150 feet long. Graham's idea was that each volunteer would claim one garden bed and tend to it. After plying me with barbequed chicken and wine that night, he'd asked me which one I'd like to tend. "I'll do all of them," I'd replied. I knew from when I gardened for my clients at the Garden of Urban that you move plants from one bed to the next to restore them. It is kind of like rearranging furniture in rooms of a house to give it a fresh new look.

My volunteer work at the pool continued months later when I was separated and living in what Graham and I later named the little house. A neighbor had rented their second home to me for $10 a month when she saw me struggling. What a blessing! I was still working in our marketing firm with my ex on the ground floor of the house I'd moved out of. I'd wake up in the little house, commute a few blocks to my ex's and my house (the big house), work with my ex, then return back to the little house at day's end. Mom was still alive at this point, but my marriage and business with my ex were transforming, and Dad's estate and safety issues with my biting dog were worrisome at best.

One day, Graham and I were moving azaleas with root balls the size of large dogs. It was ungainly and dusty work. We would dig a hole, heft the plant into it, turn it around to be at the right angle, and cover the roots up with soil. We planted one azalea together this way, and, after years and years of gardening alone, I said, "That is the first time I ever planted something with someone else."

"How did that feel?" he asked.

I choked up and said something along the lines of, "Good."

He dusted off and walked away with his battalion of little kid admirers following behind (he has a way with kids that's just magical). I sat down and wept. I knew at that instant I was at a crossroads and falling in love with him. Just months later, we'd be living together.

CHAPTER THREE:

False Starts; New Starts

We shall not cease from exploration,
and the end of all our exploring
will be to arrive where we started
and know the place for the first time.

—T.S. Eliot

Post-divorce and after my brief visit with corporate life and my Chestertown adventure, I found myself living in Graham's house as he commuted back and forth two hours each way each weekend and considering other ways to make money that didn't involve a traditional 9 to 5 J.O.B. job. It was the one piece of my life I continued to not be able to pull together. Despite my clarity of self, continued applications for employment, networking, and my ability to organize estates and house sales like a pro, I had yet to find work.

No matter how peaceful I had become with my sense of self and way of life, in my mind my self-worth was tied to my role within the working world. Graham supported much of our household, and I'd inherited some money from Mom, but solid work was elusive. And it was important. I wanted work to do.

To muddy the economic and emotional landscape at that time, there was also the potential of "winnings" from the wrongful death suit stemming from Mom's accident. The lawyer had flown from Colorado where the accident happened to take testimony from the surgeon in Arizona where Mom lived. The surgeon's professional opinion was that Mom's heart was injured by trauma from the accident and wasn't hereditary or degenerative (happening over time). We waited for over a year as the trucking company that struck the car Mom was in and Mom's lawyer agreed on a settlement amount. I was counseled not to expect a large sum of money—Mom was 75 when she died, and in this case the calculation was based on earning potential. As someone who was studying my own earning potential at the time, I found this ironic and sad.

To keep busy and make some money, I sold essential oils, as previously mentioned, and took courses in energy healing. I was coming to terms with my "Spidey-sense" and what that meant. I had also decided to honor Mom by going on an amazing adventure or two. Mom was far more adventurous than I, and this had seemed like a fitting tribute. Now, at the ripe age of 45, I decided to learn how to ride horses. Twice a week, I put my boots on and went to groom and ride horses in the Virginia hills. It was the most cathartic, peaceful way to grieve. For me, horses were more effective than the highest paid therapist.

To learn more, I volunteered at a horse rescue in Maryland. Hundreds of abused horses went through this facility every year. I mucked out stalls, groomed the horses, and turned them out to a pasture to graze. I made lots of friends—all equine. That was fine with me, since I spent most of my time crying. My horse friends leaned into me as tears rolled down my face. In the bitter cold of those January days, their breath warmed me and moistened my sweaters. It was magical. I learned the value of physical labor, and how it drew the emotion out in ways journaling and therapy couldn't seem to. I also learned something about me professionally—I liked work outside an office. Workstations and computers were not for me.

One day, I was rolling a wheelbarrow of steaming horse poop to a very large steaming pile of the same. I thought of my days two years previously at the agency I used to own with my ex. A typical day would include networking among well-dressed people, drinking coffee, talking on the phone, and sitting at my desk. Mucking out horse stalls was a massive change. I was literally moving shit around. In my mind, I was also moving shit around. There were changes going on there that only the horses knew.

As part of this horse-related grieving regimen, I booked a week-long adventure at a dude ranch with instructor Anna Twinney. She is one of the world's best horse whisperers (animal communicators, to the trade), and worked for years with the famous Monty Roberts, author of *The Man Who Listened to Horses*. He's the guy who was requested by the Queen of England to work with her horse trainers to teach them his non-violent training methods. Anna's the real deal, traveling all over the world to teach others, and I was proud she accepted me into her program.

Two things came out of this course: an expansion of my Spidey-sense, and my friendship with Marcia.

Marcia was also enrolled in the course, and we became fast friends. She is an excellent listener and also a masterful talker. I know that if I want to catch up with Marcia, I need to reserve at least two hours. She is a thorough communicator, and I love that. She went on to study with Anna for years and took many other courses to hone her craft. She makes her living now as an animal communicator, working with veterinarians hand-in-hand in Virginia, among other places.

BETH VOYLES

Cattle-cutting with Marcia.

One night at the dude ranch where we met, Marcia convinced me to compete in a cattle-cutting contest (say that five times fast after a beer or two). I often describe this as a version of tag on the front lawn, but the lawn was the size of a football field, dusty and dirt-filled, and instead of tagging each other, you had cows to rustle and horses to do the running. Teams were timed while cutting three head of cattle from the group and guiding them into a pen. A picture of Marcia and I doing this is on my Facebook page to this day. It is my kind of fun. Boy, was I proud that I stayed on my horse and rode it with some level of skill!

As part of our coursework, we worked with horses at the ranch. Anna has a long relationship with the owners, and they had selected about 40 head for our team of 10 to practice healing techniques one evening. The sun was low in the sky, and it was a cool desert night. Anna gave us some guidelines and reminded us of things we had been learning. Next, we were asked to position ourselves throughout the area. The horses would choose what happened next.

As a beginner, you doubt you have what it takes to provide any energetic help to anyone—horse, human, or otherwise. This is a silly notion, though. One just has to experience the power of touch and wordless communication with a newborn to know it works. When I talk about energy and people are doubting me, I ask folks if they have ever been crowded into an elevator and ended up moving away slightly from someone. Energy surrounds us and motivates us.

So there we were, standing on the dirt in the setting sun, waiting for a horse to select us. Horses would go from one end of the field to the other, shopping for someone,

then stop. We'd do our work with what we'd learned.
After a time, the horse would move away. Another would
approach. Sometimes, the same horse would return to us
for more. They'd indicate a spot on their bodies by moving that spot closer to our hands, and we'd work on it.
Later, we'd learn that they'd had an injury there or had
issues due to aging. To say that this experience was profound is an understatement. I struggle to put it into words
to convey how powerful it was.

ANNA I WINNEY

Doing energy work in Arizona.

I look at this adventure as a lesson not only in healing,
but in the nature of the Universe. I had a profound sense
of oneness with all things that night. We think of that con-
ceptually, but rarely *feel* it. Many people talk about this
feeling as a result of extended meditation. I got it from
standing in a field with horses—same result, different
methods. No matter how you get there, I definitely recommend it. This concept tamed my ego like none other.

I let go of having to be important. I realized I was a tiny part of a much bigger picture. It allowed me to listen differently. It changed my breathing, and how grounded I was. Granted, what I learned needed review and practice, but this experience laid a firm foundation for change within me. Beyond a college education, it is the single most important way of being to achieve success, in my opinion. It speaks volumes and has great depth.

Life isn't all high-priced games of tag and standing in a field, though, and I needed to make a living. I tried forming a little business doing energy work for a while. I had a few clients, but quickly knew that it wasn't for me. I learned that sometimes we are exposed to things as a healing process, rather than as a vocation. I remain a huge fan of the power of Reiki and other related energy modalities to heal and communicate.

Next, I fell back on my consulting and half-heartedly worked with a few folks to guide small businesses toward success. Even though I had learned previously that desk work wasn't for me, I couldn't figure out how else to perform work at the time. I'd alternate from wanting a traditional job to doing consulting with more freedom.

As if our lives weren't topsy-turvy enough, Graham and I had also decided to renovate Graham's house, top to bottom. In the space of a few months, I coordinated various contractors to replace drywall, lighting, shelving, closet configurations and doors, and handle a bit of plumbing and electrical. By the time we were done, the kitchen, both baths, laundry, office, front hall, and three bedrooms had all been reworked and redone.

During this time, Graham and I were commuting between Richmond, where he worked, and Falls Church, where his house, his high-school-age son Henry (who lived with his mom), and I were. Graham would leave in the wee hours of Monday to drive two hours south to Richmond to work—for four and a half years. We had planned to have him at that job for six months, but it was a great opportunity for him, and he thrived there. On Fridays, he would drive back north to Falls Church, me, his son, and his house. After Henry graduated from high school and moved on to college studies, I figured it would be a few months before Graham tired of the commute. After three weeks, he asked, "Why are we still coming up here?" We sold the house and moved our stuff and me closer to his work in Richmond.

Trouble was, the Richmond, Virginia, 500-square foot *pied-à-terre* apartment in which he'd been living was way too small for the two of us seven days a week. Soon, we moved again. It was not a settled time for us, our stuff, or for me.

In that we had always considered Richmond a temporary spot for Graham, we had begun thinking about where we'd like to settle permanently. Northern Virginia, where we both had lived previously, was famous then for its dense traffic and high-priced real estate and wasn't a good match. We embarked on a search for the best town for us. Like my energy work and consulting work, a home in Richmond, Virginia, didn't feel right to me. It was like a false start out of the gate. I banged up against bad matches with friends, affiliations, job opportunities, and more while we were there. It was a tremendously frustrating time of me trying to blend my way of being with new things I was learning. Like a kid who was learning how to ice skate for the first time, it was anything but smooth.

Graham is a degreed mathematician and data analyst. Before making a decision—or, ahem, deciding on a wife—he gathers what seems to me to be massive amounts of data. I see trends and feel what may be right—or, to even skip all of the above, I sense what is right and decide. As you can imagine, the latter is particularly frustrating to Graham. I have yet to compile any research to explain my instincts, so Graham usually wins out on mutual decisions with data. Thus, we began a four-and-a-half-year selection process of towns to live in next.

I was eager to move on. I was sick of false starts. Graham was hesitant to leave his job, but wanted to live in a place that met our criteria. We wanted a place with affordable real estate, less ice and snow to shovel, and that was large enough to accommodate the work he did, but small enough to not have crazy amounts of traffic. We wanted walkability, a craft-beer scene, and, ideally, a college community with art and great cafes. We toured Austin, Texas; Tampa, Florida; Charleston, South Carolina; and Asheville, North Carolina, among others.

We settled on the country's southeast region. Graham asked me to research Knoxville, Tennessee. Somehow, a website describing downtown Chattanooga neighborhoods caught my attention, and after an hour or so watching videos about everything it offered, I realized I wasn't even researching Knoxville anymore. I spent a few more hours finding out about Chattanooga. When Graham came home that night and asked about Knoxville, I told him about Chattanooga instead.

Off we went to investigate. When Graham and I went to a town to consider it, we put in hundreds of miles of driving after we got inside the city limits. We became experts in Zillow and how to assess neighborhoods and potential homes for purchase. We stayed at Airbnbs and grilled the hosts about neighborhoods, what it was like to live there, job markets, and more. Graham poured over data about water availability (we'd seen Lake Austin at record lows) and other weather and quantitative data. I looked at architecture and whether the city was making wise choices about growth.

Compared to other cities in Tennessee, Chattanooga is known for slower growth and natural beauty. *Outside Magazine* named it the best town twice—the only town to have achieved this distinction. It hasn't always been that way, though. In 1969, a Federal Air Quality report listed Chattanooga as the dirtiest city in the United States. City leaders used this as an impetus to create a cultural shift. In 1992, an aquarium—the largest fresh-water aquarium at the time—was built on the shores of the Tennessee River. It was the first of many municipal and privately funded projects to turn Chattanooga around. As a result, Chattanooga has a vibrant city center and growing economy including tech, tourism, and logistics companies. We saw that, liked it, and wanted it to be our new home.

With our decision to move to Chattanooga came what I call the Chattanooga squishy face.

"You're moving where?" the squishy faces would ask.

"To Chattanooga," we'd say.

The squishy faces would continue to look perplexed. But since our decision, *The New York Times* has written about Chattanooga as a destination twice. It is a hotspot and growing rapidly. Folks like Graham and I are flocking there. Austin was too full and expensive. So was Asheville and Nashville. We chose Chattanooga, and so did a lot of other people.

We entered the real estate market at a time when there was very little inventory. We saw a few houses, and they weren't good matches for us at all. One looked great, and we notified our realtor. She texted that the owner didn't want to show it. Houses were so popular in that area that they were selling quickly to out-of-towners like us by photographs alone. I texted our realtor: "Tell her good luck with that."

About 20 minutes later, we were packed to drive back to Richmond when we got a call. "She'll show the house for an hour." We and several other interested parties looked at the house simultaneously. We jockeyed around each other in the 100-year-old, three-bedroom, two-bath bungalow. We marveled at the big windows and plaster walls. The light was amazing. It was also priced to move—it used to be a day care center, and juice, wax, and soot clung to the walls. Cracks and nail as well as other holes were plentiful. One bedroom was painted turquoise, the other was bright neon apple green. Oh my! The rest of the house was a dark, musty, olive color. The back yard was a tangle of bushes, vines, and broken concrete. As a trained interior designer, I could look beyond all of this, but it was tough.

What captivated us was that this house was in a great part of town. The street had great trees and wasn't hilly like San Francisco, as were the surrounding blocks. When we moved the heavy blinds and shutters aside, the big windows let in beautiful light. The front porch was wide and restful. Resale value was high because of the coveted school just doors away. As some say, it had great bones, and was a good match in size for us. We were one of two bidders and were picked to negotiate for purchase.

We were out of town and the sales process was moving fast, so we got a home inspection. The report had concerning news about structure. A previous sale had folded, and maybe this was why. I got on LinkedIn and looked for a structural engineer. I kid you not, but the guy with the best credentials had a photo of himself on his LinkedIn profile with a fish on his shoulder. This was my first lesson in Chattanooga-style professionalism compared to what I was used to from Washington DC. No suit and tie for this engineer! He was qualified, but clearly had fun balancing his passions with his work life. He showed up, wrote an excellent report, and answered Graham's questions comprehensively. He assured us the structure was sound. We bought the house and prepared to move to Chattanooga, Tennessee!

Though we had been living a two-hour drive away in Richmond, Virginia, it was fitting to return to our Falls

Church, northern Virginia neighborhood, where Graham had grown up and I had lived for many years, to say goodbye. Catherine, a steadfast friend from before my divorce, was vocal about supporting Graham and me as a couple. She hosted a farewell party for us where we were able to say so long to many people we'd known from our years in the DC area. After the difficult time of my transition to being single, it was good to return and celebrate good memories. Soon after, Catherine, too, moved away—a growing trend for many of us who had lived in that neighborhood for years.

CHAPTER FOUR:

The Stuff of Life

A house is just a place to keep your stuff
while you go out and get more stuff.

—George Carlin

D o you get in your head? I do too! Have you heard the expression, "No matter where you go, there you are"? Well, there I was in Chattanooga with a multitude of worries keeping me up at night. On Facebook at 4 am, I was liking and commenting along with others, awake and restless at the same ungodly hour. The day began with coffee, and I'd jangle along, trying to be calm about the recent move we'd made. I had hopes, but not firm beliefs, that the new life we were embarking upon would go along just dandy. I was a worrier and one with a vivid imagination, so I struggled in my new spot, even though I chose it. The

stuff we'd left behind in Virginia didn't include the stuff
in my head. That was clearly and vividly still there.

I'd like to say that my self-discovery post-divorce was
peacefully putting me at one with the Universe, but it
wasn't. I aimed for resilience upon change, but did not
achieve it. I truly admire people who can bounce back
from events with nary a memory or a scratch. I am not
one of them. In my first months in Chattanooga, I struggled. Though we had moved with less clutter in our truck,
somehow clutter had filled my mind. I desperately wanted
the peaceful and balanced life I'd enjoyed in Chestertown.
Instead, I was challenged to draw upon my resources to
use what I'd learned during those beautiful days on the
Chesapeake instead.

As my sounding board, Graham was a saint, but one
with human limitations. He'd listen to me about how I
was taking up space, existing here on Earth with no purpose as a completely useless blob. He eventually gave up
and agreed with me for a while. He, like all of us, has
a dark side, and his is extremely critical—with data to
prove it. It was horrible. I began looking for apartments
for me and our dog and was more lost than ever. Our
whole dream of building a life together in a new place of
our choosing was set aside, scrapped, and tossed when we
reached our destination.

In addition to being sad and overly analytical, I also
was pissed. I had coordinated the redesign of Graham's
house, which helped the sale tremendously. I was a patient
mate as he worked in Richmond for well beyond the ini-
tial, six-month plan. I'd also worked hard to lighten our

load and combine our belongings into one cohesive home that made sense. The reduction of stuff took years. I didn't plan on taking years to deal with all of those belongings, but I did. For me and many others, the first step we use to get our lives in order is to get their physical world in order. The second step, like construction, was to build a life to suit our needs—in our case, in Chattanooga. What I didn't know then was that this would form the basis of my future work and way of living at home—a life of minimalism, wise choices, and beauty.

Miraculously, we were able to move to Tennessee with one U-Haul truck. We towed my car behind us, and Fred sat between us on a pile of dog beds and blankets. So what had I gone through to get our belongings into one 18-foot truck? Like many Americans after a divorce, I had piles of stuff, and I had to get rid of it to be able to move on to the next step. Not only did I have the remains from my dad's estate, but I also had the household items from me and my ex (he was smart enough to move to New York City with only what he needed for an apartment). Computers, furniture, office equipment, and supplies from our branding agency filled multiple boxes. Dad's estate included the objects from my grandparents on that side too—conveniently stored in their entirety in five garden sheds behind Dad's mobile home. This was soon to be joined by the contents of Graham's house (we had duplicate items such as coffee makers, printers, etc.), objects from my mom's estate, and, soon after, items from Graham's mom's estate. All in all, we handled five dead people's stuff and the contents from a 1,500-square-foot office. That's a lot for an only child of two only children. Suddenly, I was surrounded by lots of people's stuff. As a minimalist who yearns for clean architectural lines, I didn't like this at all.

Stuff is trash and easy to deal with if it is of no monetary or sentimental value. If it fits into either of those categories though, you have to make hard choices.

Of great sentimental value were almost 100 scarves I inherited from both Mom and Dad. Dad had a bunch of Liberty of London classic printed beauties that were now mine. I loved all 100 but even as an avid scarf wearer, did not need that many. I didn't want to sell them because of their sentimental value. So I developed a plan: whichever girlfriends answered the phone one afternoon and answered my question would get a set of scarves mailed to them. "What is your favorite color?" I'd ask when they said hello. If it was blue, a set of blue scarves would go in a padded envelope with their address on it right away. At the end of a few fun phone calls, I was about 40 scarves lighter.

The best example of moving stuff with no monetary value was all of Dad's cars. Years before, I'd had to fill out a 40-page form to get Dad registered for Medicaid. He couldn't qualify because he owned eight cars. My job at the time was to prove that all eight cars were worthless. Stuff is stuff if it has no monetary or sentimental value. Believe me, I found no sentimental value in those junkers.

Since dealing with eight cars at once, I learned a bounty of tricks and tips to deal with excess stuff. The first and most important one is this: if it has no value to you, get rid of it. It may have monetary value or value to a gift giver, friend, workmate, or relative, but if it has no value to you, out it goes. Try selling it or finding it a new home! The amount of stuff we keep because it has some value is astounding. Just because it is worth something doesn't mean it needs to live with you for decades. Would we live with someone we couldn't stand? Probably not. But Uncle Walter's toaster that we saw one time on that Facebook page of collectables . . . better keep it forever in the garage!

The second trick is to develop a staging area. When you wade through stuff like we were, it was important to have space to box things up, move things out, and otherwise sort and pack.

Before doing anything, I sorted things into categories. For example, all the office equipment went together, all the barware, all the music, and so on. This was especially important for us selling online. Invariably people ask if there are any more like what you just sold. They don't want to hear that you may or may not have more, depending what is in the other unsorted piles. One day, I sold a Kate Spade purse I no longer used. The same person bought half the other purses too. If your goal is to move stuff out, this works incredibly well.

Next, I determined how long I'd wait to sell something. If you have all week/ month/ year, price it for what you think it is worth. I wanted it to sell quickly, so I priced it for slightly less. People felt like they got a good deal; I got more room to live in. It's a win-win. I remember showing Lise a cubic foot of space that I had created in our home by selling a bunch of stuff that used to occupy that space.

She is more patient than I am and was considering selling things for what they were worth. For me, that space was worth more to me than having what I sold. I wanted to live in that space, not be hampered down by possessions someone else had selected and that I didn't want. It was time to move on!

The third trick I learned was timing. Generally, when folks are timed, they focus and move along quickly. For sorting and moving stuff, it worked well. My magic number was 20 minutes. I'd set an egg timer and told myself I could take a break after 20 minutes. Nine times out of ten, I worked sorting stuff well beyond the 20 minutes because I was on a roll.

Another trick we learned was to digitize whenever possible. We now have a handy collection of music, all accessible by phone, that used to be on CDs. For photographic prints and slides, Graham literally sorted them into large Hefty garbage bags. If it was a random picture of a hill or the Arc de Triomphe, out it went. The rest, with pictures of our family, were saved and digitized.

Despite horror stories of early digitizing companies shipping treasured family photographs by boat off to foreign lands to scan, I gave it a try. Sure enough, it was a five-month process of locating my photos and getting the scans. Eventually, all the photographs were returned to us along with five handy CDs (now themselves old technology too), and all was well.

One day, I separated a portfolio of representative work from samples of graphic design we used to give to clients from the branding agency. What I threw away filled seven recycle bins. I sat on the curb and cried. I didn't know what else to do. Thirteen years of work and memories sat there in recycle bins. That chapter of my life was over.

Another time, I tangled with the Mercedes that I inherited from my mom. I swear that every time I drove that thing, it cost me $400. Even simple repairs cost $400. Compared to my new Hyundai, it just wasn't measuring up. Her car must have heard me because one night before heading to work, it woke me with horns blaring and lights flashing. It was like Christine from the Stephen King novel—a car possessed. I took good pictures, placed an ad, and sold that car to the first person who took it for a test drive.

As I listed items for sale, met with potential buyers, negotiated prices, and more, I thought about what I'd do once all of this stuff was out of my life. I had dreams of doing more with less. What inspired me was the thought of how small a house we could fit into by having less stuff requiring closets and shelves. What also inspired me was making choices for myself about what stuff I liked and wanted in my life. I was moved to select items that were relevant to whom I had become. We also could use our earnings for time away from work, experiences such as travel and good eating, and wise choices like retirement savings.

What hit me was the clarity I had from owning less. I was stripped of my marriage, home, dog, family, and job—all within three years. In the time that followed, I got rid of more, organized more, and processed. I sat with the piles and cried. I sorted. I cried some more. I met great people and sold them things. I cried some more. From this, I got clarity. Was it fast? No. Was I resilient, bouncing back painlessly? Nope. I had the luxury of time to process mountains of stuff that I'd inherited through all that loss.

The biggest item to sort out was my house with my ex. The property was a mid-century modern gem with great park views, an amazing lot, and pretty gardens. With my interior design background, I'd redone the whole thing from top to bottom, complete with outdoor shower, deck overlooking the park, wine refrigerator, and all the trimmings. But it was 2009. Nothing was selling. Houses were foreclosing in record numbers. We needed to make a certain amount to cover the mortgage and other obligations. We set the price accordingly, considerably higher than what nearby houses were selling for at the time. We developed a market approach and waited. The first good sign was that two hundred brochures were taken, one by one, from a little plastic box at the end of the driveway.

One day, I was walking our dog, and someone I'd never met approached me. "You'll never sell that house for that ridiculous amount. Never!" she hissed.

I have no idea how I did this, but I leaned even closer to her. "Watch me," I said quietly. The house sold two weeks later for tens of thousands above market rate. Though my ex and I were divorcing and selling our house, we continued to work together for clients for a time. We were good at what we did. Do not underestimate the power of two owners of an award-winning branding agency to market and sell a great-looking piece of real estate. It was and still is a spectacular property.

Artwork was a whole other category of significant things that needed sorting. My parents divorced in 1977 and continued to trade art back and forth between themselves for years, with me as a broker in between. Not counting the art from Mom's estate, we moved 53 framed pieces of art into Graham's house. The volume was staggering.

Cath as a young girl among some of her parent's art

We did not have enough wall space to house 53 works of art. It was definitely a first-world problem, but at the time we were both unemployed, and would rather spend our time and energies on finding work. Eventually, a compromise of sorts was reached: move the art along and try to make money from it while looking for work at the same time. In an effort to cull and give good homes to the art and not just sell it to strangers, we began what we named The Art Relocation Project in earnest. Enter stage right: Michele and Michelle. I had grown to know them both through Landmark Education and had enjoyed many late nights of shared secrets and dreams. They were incredibly kind, generous, and supportive of every new avenue I tried. They listened as I fell on my knees with grief. I was so glad to know them both. Fortuitously, they also had walls in need of art. They were at a point in their decorating lives beyond posters, but weren't ready to pay for a whole house of real paintings. We transported canvasses to both their homes and hung each with care. It is so much fun to visit them and see old art friends. It is also good to know the art has found a good home.

There was other art that I had brought from Dad's mobile home and kept. Graham and I were considering one to hang in the bedroom and checked the artist before committing to have the frame repaired. After a web search, Graham said, "Come here and see this. The artist just had his studio in Australia redone and paid for by the Getty Museum." Dad had always said that piece was worth something. We quickly looked at the origins of the other art pieces from his mobile home. The collection was a top-10 list of hits of 1970s artists from Western Australia, with one representative piece from each artist. The artists had creatively fed and profited off each other and had become collectable— in Australia. I figured out about international shipping, art-handling, and Australian auctions, and lived off the proceeds for months. It was a windfall at a precious time when I needed funds badly. He might not have paid for my education, but Dad came through after the divorce with art!

Besides art, there were far less glamorous items like furniture, appliances, rugs, and all else. I became the Queen of Craigslist. It was amazing to see the parade of Mercedes, BMWs, and other name-brand cars whose drivers came to buy our stuff. It allowed me to pay off a bunch of debt too—thank God. I've rarely, if ever, used credit cards since.

One day, a gal came to buy the plants we'd found in the dumpster. They had grown to six-foot stunners, and were now in great pots to show off their fabulous form. She and I stood in the driveway talking for almost an hour. Similarly, yesterday I spent two hours talking to a dear friend that I met on Instagram. Ah, the power of social media to connect people. Well, after the plant buyer and I talked for an hour and shared our stories with each other, she said, "May I hug you? I feel like we need to say goodbye in a better way than me just getting in my car." We hugged, and as I walked up the driveway alone, I reflected on how selling things can connect people. We often don't like to be sold to, but if it is something that is dear and treasured, it is a whole other conversation between new friends.

If you think about it, we are all sales people at one time or another. We sell the concept of being together for the future when we propose marriage. We sell the concept that the dinner is really delicious when it is kind of so-so. We sell our capabilities when we interview for a job. It is an art of convincing, educating, sharing, and discovering for your audience.

I've been in sales in one form or another since 1995. When people get good and snobby about it, I remind them that the fourth major source of millionaires in America is sales people and sales consultants. Sales is only a dirty word if you don't need anything or anybody. If that is how you think, good luck with that solitary existence. The rest of us are being sold to in one form or another.

I learned a lot about sales in my driveway loading Craigslist items into trunks. I learned about what sold, how it sold, and who it sold to. I learned more about sales frequency, speed, and volume than I had in years. I learned to enjoy the person-to-person interaction. I got hugs! This was an important lesson in that I had a strong showing of J tendencies in the Myers-Briggs Personality Type Indicator (MBTI). If you are not familiar with it, this is a tool used by HR and psychology folks to assess people and their behavior.

Basically, J stands for judging—not like a judge in court, but rather in the tendency to want closure, rather than gathering possibilities, called perceiving, or P, tendencies. In dating, a P person would say, "I'll call you." We J people wouldn't be comfortable with that at all. We'd want to know when and have some closure on that preamble! In sales, people with J tendencies tend to want a buying decision quickly.

Riding the bus and $30 grocery budgets gave me a new perspective about sales and my role in the process. I had a vulnerability that used to show itself in bravado, ego, and quick-decision mentality. Now, in my new self-appointed sales position in the driveway, I had time to listen to why the object that someone was buying was important to them. I heard stories of growing house-holds, new beginnings, collections, other great bargains, and love. It was a tremendous honor to witness. I helped them grow, in a way, and really enjoyed it. I thought a lot about the scale of what I was selling. In my former role, I sold design work ranging from a thousand dollars to over eighty-thousand. Now I was discussing items around $50. The relationships were different and more intimate at this level. It comforted me.

For myself, selling all that stuff gave me space. It literally was space where an object used to be, but also a beginning of space in my cluttered mind for what needed attention. It allowed me to think about what I wanted out of life and where I wanted to make that happen. Around this time, Graham and I began our research of places to live. I started by practicing this clarity exercise on objects, but I soon graduated to situations. I grew to have a sense of self and awareness that I hadn't had before. Coming home from my hiatus on the Chesapeake Bay wasn't so bad after all.

About three months before we left Richmond to live in Chattanooga, I returned to Craigslist to fill the void of time. I had tired of consulting and just wanted to be "out there working, doing something useful." Maybe Craig-slist would have the perfect three-month gig. I applied for one job. It was for seasonal, part-time work in garden centers, selling plants. It didn't say which garden center

or what plants, but I filled out the form with my gardening credentials from my Garden of Urban gardening
company I had while in grad school, my time teaching
science through gardening with kids, and my Master
Gardener Certification.

They wanted me to try a management job, but I asked
instead to be with the college kids at the entry level on the
sales floor. Graham took me to his favorite store to buy
the solid boots required for the job. I moved my three-
inch heels for sales presentations to boards of directors
further into the back of my closet.

I'd considered being in a garden center before. I knew
that desk work didn't make me happy. I knew that I loved
to garden. But I was embarrassed to have my friends and
neighbors see me working retail. I was afraid of the rid-
icule and perceived whispered words behind my back. I
held myself away from the possibility of working in a garden center because I was embarrassed.

My new boss's former position was in the Army. He
was no joke and expected us to move fast. I lost weight
like there was no tomorrow. I came home and slept like
the dead. I loved it and laughed loud and long with my
coworkers. I loved my workmates, the plants, the customers, the environment—the whole deal. It was the first time
I had ever loved my work on a sustained basis. Sure, there
were many times when I had achieved things or projects
came together, and they were amazing. I loved those
moments, but I had a lifetime of hated jobs. God bless
the people who know what they want to be at a young
age. I didn't, yet I had a work ethic that guided me to

work tirelessly for long hours. It was a nasty combination of wanting to work badly, yet hating my various jobs and professions year after year after year.

It wasn't an official function of the company, but we'd begin the day singing together while placing hundreds of plants on shelves. I loved this and taught the college kids a few 80s hits. We practically wet our pants doing Devo imitations with colored flower pots on our heads. During all this singing and hilarity, plants were going from a large cart to flat, open areas. We often threw the gallon pots from a cart to the person who was placing them on the shelves. I was born with a deformity in my eyes, and, as a result, my eyes don't work together, resulting in no depth perception. This makes any sport with a ball (or flying flower pot) tremendously challenging. The nice thing about a gallon potted plant flying through the air is that it is substantially larger than a ball. Ninety-nine percent of the time, I caught them and placed plants in attractive rows in record time. My confidence grew, and Graham really liked that. He'd been quietly rooting for me, staying in the background and watching me learn about myself, define myself, and learn to love myself. He was proud of me.

When we weren't tossing or hauling at the garden center, we were interfacing with customers. There could be a row of six of us in one area, and a customer would walk up to me for the answer to a question. This happened numerous times, and we garden center folk laughed about it. The days of working with my Craigslist customers must have shone through. It kept me busy, and I learned to pace myself. The days blew by. I loved my job and wasn't embarrassed to say so. I was proud of my work for the first time in my life.

Soon, it was time to move to our newfound home in Chattanooga. I had to leave my job, but applied for a position in the same company at another garden center just north of our new house. It was a logical next step using my Garden of Urban experience as well as my more recent work slinging pots with the coeds. I was sad to leave my new friends, but knew that we were moving to a town that better suited our needs.

CHAPTER FIVE:

Community
for Better or Worse

Community is a place where the connections
felt in our hearts make themselves known
in the bonds between people,
and where the tuggings and pullings
of those bonds keep opening our hearts.

—Parker J. Palmer

When I moved to Chattanooga, I had no friends there, but thankfully six dear ones available via telephone. As Graham and I renovated our new house from its daycare center former existence, I called them for relief and laughs. I needed them. Graham and I weren't getting along and were fighting horribly. I was miserable, sad, and lonely, questioning whether our search for a new home made any sense at all. We had a nasty dose of buyers' remorse and wondered if Chattanooga was the right town for us. It was a cultural shift, and we weren't prepared for the differences.

As with any move, it took time to meet new people. As we patched plaster and painted trim, I thought about friendship and community and how to find it.

Soon after I'd divorced and before my six dear friends entered my life, I'd taken a course where we were asked to lay out a diagram of our circles of community. I'd shown mine to a trusted adviser (OK, therapist) at the time, and he'd said, "Cath, this is really sad." We'd spent the session acknowledging that I had little or no community surrounding me.

What I realized then and later, while painting in Chattanooga, was that I hadn't made very many friends in my life. I could blame that on moving 17 times (or 26, depending how you figure it) or my lack of friend-making skills. Also, not having a firm self-identity presented a mixed bag for potential friends, so I bet it was confusing to be around me. I yearned for the kind of friend you make in a sorority or as life-long neighbors playing in the park. It may have been idyllic, but I wanted what I didn't have.

What I had was a collection of drinking buddies, vendors who catered to my needs, and folks who knew me by convenience such as neighbors, workmates, and membership-based affiliations. But when it came down to it, I lacked the true-blue friends who would show up if I were in trouble. My chart was eerily empty. Lise, though from my and Graham's old Northern Virginia neighborhood, had yet to become a friend at the time of this course. I had also yet to befriend Michelle and Michele, who actually became my friends through this course where I made the diagram. Jayne, from that first moment when she offered to pack my kitchen, was a lifelong compatriot, but our years that solidified our relationship had yet to occur.

After this realization, I didn't set off to find likely candidates. Instead, I chose to hate myself. As a recent divorcee, I had reason to believe I was unlovable and unkind too. Yuck. I was such a joy to be around—ha ha. I went through hell. Graham, who was also new to Chattanooga and friendless and without work yet, got to live with me. Oh, the joy we had that year!

When I'd sold essential oils, I'd made one friend called Gigi. She was a teacher of a course, about essential oil history and uses, that I had travelled to Norfolk/Virginia Beach area to take. After class the first day, we found we were staying at the same guest house. I watched her pack her suitcase for over three hours and remember shaking as we talked about the most amazing things the entire time. After class the next day, she returned to Colorado, and I drove north to Richmond. For two years afterwards, we became incredibly close friends by telephone. When I finally saw her for the second time, I blurted out, "You are so short!" I didn't really know what she looked like! Though only meeting twice in person, Gigi remains one of my best friends to this day.

What had increased my odds of making friends in the past? I thought about it and remembered my numerous hours of volunteering. I recalled my dog foster friends who'd stood together with available dogs each weekend at the big-box pet supply store. Though some people probably thought we were crazy, what we really were was a great community of dog lovers. We continue to be in touch via Facebook to trade dog advice. I got plenty of human advice from them too. At Christmas, we'd dust the dog hair off our favorite sweaters and gather for good cheer. I treasured that early, supportive group. Whether we stood on two legs or four, we were well-intentioned and gathered around a good cause. If my fellow dog-lovers only knew how badly I needed them at the time.

As usual, Graham was a good sport about my dog fostering. After we placed a dog with an adopter, I'd get another one or two. Graham never knew what size and shape companion would get out of the car with me on those days. One was part-wolf. He stunk up the whole house. Thankfully, I only had him for a weekend. Others were stubborn, afraid, or lonely. We dealt with hiding under the bed, fear of leaving the house, food aggression, and a host of other dog issues. We learned how to build dog confidence so that, once a person fell in love with them, they'd be a strong, happy, viable canine companion.

Our final foster we'd adopted moved to Chattanooga with us. He was called Fred. Fred. Seriously? Who'd name a dog Fred? We didn't have a foster at that time because we were travelling back and forth between Richmond and DC each week. We heard about Fred the dog, who needed to be placed quickly, and I talked with the placement coordinator. I was quiet at the dinner table after that, and Graham asked, "You want to foster another dog, don't you?" A few minutes and texts later, I was planning to meet at the nearby grocery store parking lot for a handoff.

We met, and Nancy, the coordinator, said of the owner, "I've never seen a man cry giving up a dog like that. He was wearing a leather jacket, and it was all wet from tears." This kind of story happens as dogs move back and forth, so I heard it, looked at Fred, and prepared to drive home with him to see what happened next. As I drove, I thought of the man's wet leather jacket. I recalled the tears I had shed with all the deaths in my recent past, the divorce, and struggles to find work. I recalled my poor dog Beatrice and how she didn't make it. This guy's tears and mine, and the movement of animals and their persons' lives, all blended in my mind. We aren't so different, you and I—we are of one mourning body, I thought. Meanwhile, Fred, my new foster, waited patiently in the hatchback of my car to find new shelter in my home.

We dutifully went to try to place Fred at several adoption events. Fred is an American Staffordshire Terrier (aka pit bull) and very mellow. When he'd meet potential families, he'd put himself in a sit before them and wait quietly for potential adopters to pet him. He reminded me of a butler in an old black-and-white film, waiting by the door for instructions. In my opinion, he was an amazing, well-mannered gentleman, a breed ambassador.

Fred's good manners weren't the best sales technique, though. Time and again, the boisterous and eager pitties would head home with new families. We'd head home to our foster home together, promising Fred better luck the following week. What we hadn't realized yet is that Fred was a dear, quiet and loyal friend to us. In among the moving, renovations, and turmoil of settling estates, he was a constant companion, a lovebug and confidante.

After a time, our neighbors across the street fell in love with him, and we prepared to give Fred away. In that we'd placed 12 other dogs, we were familiar with the sadness. We'd placed another dog, Jasmine, with our

Fred at home

other across-the-street neighbor and were excited to have a whole cul-de-sac of former fosters. But giving away Fred felt different. I was beyond sad. I was losing a family member. I wimped out and made Graham call the neighbor to tell them they couldn't have him. Fred remains with us to this day and is sleeping here at my feet as I write. Our little family now had a dog of our very own. Since Graham and I weren't married or committed to each other forever yet, this was a big step to take.

How else had I found community? In 1988, at the height of the AIDS epidemic, I found community amongst the survivors. We volunteered together for The NAMES Project AIDS Memorial Quilt. People were dying in the prime of their lives. We would go to a funeral a week. Joe, who sat next to me at work; Mark, my college roommate's brother; Richard, the head of our school club—the list went on and on. We remembered their names and honored them. AIDS was everywhere.

As I volunteered on the Quilt, I remember my cheek muscles hurting. Despite the grief, there was so much life there. My cheek muscles hurt from smiling so much.

After volunteering for one national display, I got a call from Mike Smith, one of the key founders of the Quilt. When he identified himself on the phone, I said, "Sure, it's Mike Smith. Now tell me another." Well, it was him, and he asked me to serve as the National Volunteer Coordinator for the next national display. Oh, my. I stuffed my words inside my mouth and answered his questions.

Later, in 1993, I was tapped again to gather over 200 volunteers in less than a week. This was before everyone had email, so several hundred phone calls later, we had our volunteers to bring the Quilt to Bill Clinton's Inaugural Parade. Our group marched almost last on that dreadfully cold January day. The Clintons and Gores were still in their observation booth at the White House, waving at us as we walked past with panels honoring the dead. This community had far-reaching effects.

Community surrounds us, for better or worse. If you are lucky, community permeates your home and you make friends that are dear to you. For some reason, with these communities and others, I hadn't met what some people call their tribe. Since I was a kid, I saw groups bond and become close. I was often the outsider or new kid in town. Yes, there were people in these groups that I knew who knew me. None had been identified as, groomed to be, or grown into dear, close friends at all. At this point in my life, post-divorce in 2010, I wanted friends with a capital F. People to stand by me if I ever got married again. People who would hold my hand if I fell mortally ill. People to house me if my home burned down. Those kind of friends. In many ways, not finding myself amongst friends was something that stopped me from thriving personally for decades. This was compounded by my tiny family and lack of community among relatives.

Many of us deal with family that is less than ideal, so we reach out and find community and friends elsewhere. The point I'm making here is that for most of my life, I either didn't have the opportunity because I was moving soon, or because I was horrible at making friends. As a result, I spent most of my life being lonely. In a "hindsight is 20/20 vision" sort of way, I realized that this probably contributed to lack of success in my first marriage.

What was it about the process of divorcing, grieving, and selling my stuff that allowed me to learn to make friends? I was literally doing more with less. I dove head-long into the Zen way of being: truly having very little and being open to infinite possibility. The first round was seeing new ways to relate to people and have dear friends that I'd waited decades to meet.

The second round, that I had yet to realize, was in finding fulfillment at work. At that point, I had no idea what that was going to bring. All I knew was that getting rid of old stuff felt good, and that my best choice was to keep trudging on!

I truly believe that clearing my head and getting rid of physical stuff around me gave me space to make friends. It freed me to not be attached to belongings and status, but rather focus on the people in front of me and love them in a whole new way. As I look back, I know the massive amounts of mental clutter there prevented community around me. Shorthand I've since learned is: clutter within . . . community without. Put another way: if you don't have your mental house in order, it is doubtful that folks will want to hang out with you while you live that way. Truly yucky, deep, dark stuff, not meant to be written down here or anywhere, got in the way of people getting near me. I can't say I blame them either!

Happily, I also had a much better sense of who I was. I had a more defined product to sell on the friends market, per se. Because of the massive amount of self-examination, misfortune, and self-discovery I'd gone through, I was vulnerable in a way I'd never been before in my life. Gone was my need to be respected and liked. I just was who I was, warts and all. I was ready to be embarrassed (again) because I'd been so ashamed.

CHAPTER SIX:

Learning to Listen

*There is a difference between listening
and waiting for your turn to speak.*

—Simon Sinek

In the three years or so prior to moving to Chattanooga, I'd learned to listen ... better. Part of this came from my clearing the space in my mind to hear. The discipline I developed was to be still while someone else is talking—truly still and quiet, both within and without. I also stopped waiting to respond and, instead, would be with someone as they communicated. As a result, I rarely am prepared to answer. I'm not thinking of a response when someone else is talking. It makes me seem slow and unprepared, but that's me listening. Last, I lost my agenda and was more grounded in what was in the present, no matter how badly that appeared. Beginning while on my hiatus to Chestertown, I learned the power of taking stock in the present and appreciating what exists. It is also me learning to listen—it will be a lifelong pursuit!

It is my belief that coming out of myself, letting go of a bit of control, being vulnerable, and developing better listening skills really helped me be a better friend. So at long last, I gathered a little tribe. I thanked God I'd found Graham, Jayne, Michele, Michelle, Lise, Marcia, and Gigi. They are my people. Added to them are about 20 other folks who are dear to me and with whom I routinely stay in touch. All I needed were a few near me in Chattanooga.

When I was 10 or so years old, Mom travelled often and left me with friends for weeks while she was away. One of these caretakers was named Marilyn, and I adored her. She saw me and got me in ways I hadn't experienced before. As someone that was young, this was an early, profound experience. Marilyn said I was a sensitive person. I have since learned about highly sensitive people, read books on that topic, and can relate to much of what they describe.

I believe that many of us sensitive types are mis– diagnosed with various ailments as a result of our ways of receiving information. In my case, I was diagnosed with chronic depression. It makes sense—I was always the new kid in town, the lonely only child, and sensitive. Beginning somewhere around age 14, I was told I was limited by this condition. I believed them. Can you imagine being told you are depressed and that you'd never get over it as a chronic condition, forever? I was. Later in a mismatched marriage hoping for something better, I again was told I was depressed. For 15 years, I took a variety of anti-depressant drugs. Since childhood, I wasn't open or listening for other ways to address what I was told I had medically. I just plunked along, sad about a chronic condition.

By the time I was sharing that small apartment in Richmond with Graham, I was ready for new things and was listening differently to my body, health, and what was possible for me. I was in love with Graham and had new hope about living my life in a new way. Also, Graham was a particularly good listener and kind about coaching me when I was failing miserably both at listening and at having hope about ever feeling better consistently.

One afternoon, I attended a professional networking function and overheard someone talking about a nurse practitioner who prayed with you after your first session together. I'd never heard of faith being part of the healing process, but knew from portrayals in art history that this wasn't a new idea. I decided to give this medical office a try. After 17 pages of forms, a two-hour intake session, and 12 vials of blood for various tests, I was convinced that prayer was just *part* of her strategy.

The key discovery was that I wasn't depressed. I had normal levels of serotonin and a number of other scientific indicators of balanced mental health. What I lacked were a number of vitamins and minerals and had a massive amount of toxins in my body. For the first time, we were listening to data instead of listening to stories and words.

This isn't to say therapy isn't appropriate sometimes, but we do blood tests for lots of other things, why not for this?

In short, my sensitivities to these toxins were shutting me down. An example of how this shutting down affected my life is that I would often spend one entire day a week napping, usually Saturdays. Can you imagine losing one entire day a week or more? I did for years.

We began a six-month detox process. She warned that I would often feel like I had the flu and she was right. For six months, off and on, I felt like I had the flu. The result was substantially fewer toxins in my body, and, bit by bit, I felt like I had more energy, health, and vitality. My sex life vastly improved. I felt better. I still get frustrated and angry and dislike the darker, short days of winter, but I am not the depressed person I once was. And best of all, I don't have the expense or responsibility to medicate myself daily with pills I didn't need. This isn't for everybody, but it was the right path for me. Get good medical advice. It can't be beat!

Mental health is a hot topic in the US, particularly with gun violence. It is tough to be lumped in with those who potentially might shoot a bunch of people. Those of us who get sad are much, much less likely to be mass killers than people might think after watching the news. Shooting and sadness are two completely different things. For me, I'd get incredibly sad if I were contemplating killing several classmates. But I digress.

Just because I discontinued anti-depressants didn't mean I was happy all the time. Like normal people, I feel a range of emotions, including sadness. What I learned from my sadness since not taking anti-depressants is that much of it is situational. It comes, it goes, and if I'm smart, I let it have its time and work through it with support of an intimate community of those who love me.

Graham was an integral part of me taking responsibility for my emotions and taking the step not to be medicated. Right after we moved to Chattanooga and we weren't getting along, this process was bumpy at best, but I continued on anyway. Graham, too, had mental housecleaning work to do and did it. It helped our relationship immeasurably. So did good old communication. We talked for hours on ways we could be together more successfully. Good relationships are worth the work, in my opinion, and work we did.

After Graham and I decided to stay together, we worked consistently on ways to listen to each other more effectively. I, in turn, learned to listen to myself more effectively and not burden Graham with every sticky weirdness I was trying to sort out. Because of this shift, my six key girlfriends got more phone calls to assist. I, in turn, was a resource to them to resolve their dark moments. We are there for each other when life deals out unjust situations, health issues arise, bills seem insurmountable, and more. With the power of new friends and listening techniques, I was able to keep my relationship together.

For extra-credit staying together points, Graham and I decided to embark upon a four-month renovation of six rooms of our new Chattanooga home. Not the smartest maneuver, but that's what we decided. To add to this rocky time, I decided to pursue full-time work again rather than the seasonal work offered at the garden center affiliate of the one I'd worked with in Richmond. Graham was happy to focus on renovations after the incredibly stressful government job he'd left in Richmond, but I wanted to find full-time work badly. To complicate things, I completely ignored all that I'd learned about my love of not working at a desk and had applied to a whole mass of corporate desk jobs I didn't want.

Nothing had changed from the last time I'd edited my resume (other than my beloved garden center gig with the coeds), so I still had my mixed bag of skills. I had added multi-level marketing and consulting to the "tried everything" menu, netting no results. Other potential hiring red flags were my being an entrepreneur since 1995 and a woman in her fifties.

They say there isn't age discrimination, but I believe it exists. Clues abound such as "two years' experience in X"—what if you have 20? Often the thinking is that people my age don't understand social media. Communication, despite the media, is communication, no matter what your age. Since that time, I have gained a following in social media and have taught classes to eager (and often decades younger) people about social media strategy and techniques. Touché, good people!

Pursuing corporate communications work at that time was a vivid example of me not listening to myself and what made me happy. I ignored my success and happiness in my garden center work to pursue something that I had hated for years. This was true situational depression by my own doing. No, I didn't return to antidepressant pills. Instead, I wailed massive tears and wondered if I had any worth on Earth. I felt like a miserable waste of a human taking up space and not having a role in society. That mixture of work ethic and not getting work reared its head and bit me with a vengeance.

In years past, in situations like this I'd call my mother. "Mom, I can't find work," I'd say, or something along those lines. Invariably in calls like that we'd end up talking about Mom's new glasses or her exercise class. We'd talk about me and my woes for a bit, but her main angle was to talk about something else—and fast. I figured this out in my forties and would try to guide her back into my malaise. No go. Mom would have none of that. Life was too short for that shit, and she wouldn't have it. Off she'd go, with a big laugh.

While I was applying for communications jobs in Chattanooga, I remembered when Mom was my rock after I'd been shortlisted 19 times for communications positions back in Northern Virginia years before. She weathered that roller coaster ride with me day in and day out. When I got that job years before, it was like we'd both landed it together. During one of those roller coaster calls, she stopped me. "Listen!" she commanded. "You can move mountains!" She believed it and believed in me. She just didn't want to hear my troubles. When I get down and my girlfriends or Graham aren't around, I cling to that idea that I can move mountains. It has helped me repeatedly since.

After applying for a bunch of jobs in Chattanooga with no luck, I gave up. Sure, you can run a whole communications agency in DC, but no, you will not be given the opportunity to do the work of one communications professional here in Tennessee. To say I was discouraged and probably prevented anyone from hiring me was an understatement. Framed another way, I wasn't listening to myself and what I wanted out of life. Some people would say the Universe was talking to me, in that there was one roadblock after another and absolutely no flow. Either way, this communications professional was getting a lesson in listening!

After having been in Chattanooga for six months with no luck finding professional communications work, I applied for a job to fill the days with a home design/big-box store needing Christmas help. Again, I was working alongside college kids. This time, though, I didn't like it. A group of us would typically unpack hundreds of boxes to get merchandise out of packing material and ready for the shelves. On those days, I'd come home and soak my hands in ice water. It was painful to open my share of hundreds of boxes day after day. Other days, I was sent to the floor to merchandise. I would stuff product on shelves at that busy Christmas season with the best of them. On slower days, I'd learn about merchandising. It was a part of marketing I'd never been exposed to. I knew about advertising, branding, sales, marketing, and public affairs, but had never been exposed to merchandising. It was part science and part art—a really interesting combination to me. But the job was a bad match, and at the end of the Christmas season, I was happy to leave.

Soon after my home décor/big-box stint, my friends

Dawn and Derek visited us to look at real estate in Chattanooga. We began our visit by showing them all Graham's and my gardening projects. The back yard had been cleared of over two tons of vines and concrete, and a new garden was in place. The front bed was also freed of vines and a menacing carpet of ornamental liriope grass and now had a perennial bed in place. An oak tree graced the other side of the yard and shaded our beloved front porch where a porch swing hung. We outlined plans for the side bed we were saving to work on later. We were very proud to show off our accomplishments, and Dawn and Derek listened patiently.

After the tours of our gardens we got organized, and I shuttled them around and showed them various neighborhoods in the area. Derek was a customer of our communications agency in DC, and I'd stayed in touch in the years since. He, like other former clients, knew my work habits and how I wove them into entrepreneurial efforts. "There were talented designers there, but it was you that made that firm a success, Cath," he told me. "You need to do your own thing. I think you need to open a garden center. You talk about gardening all the time."

I laughed at him. What a preposterous idea.

Dismissing is another form of not listening. Subconsciously, though, I heard him. During my explorations with Dawn and Derek, I'd seen a piece of property for auction. It had a small building and a fence around it—perfect for keeping the plants safe at night. I tucked that idea away for days, walked the dog, and got quiet. I was torn and trying my best to listen to forces larger than me.

"What is an appropriate next step?" I asked. I waited in the silence.

Three days later, I couldn't stand it anymore. "Graham, can you come look at something with me?" He got in the car, not a question asked. What a guy! He had no idea. We pulled up to the property, which was covered in trash with weeds everywhere. Across the street were three boarded-up buildings. Next door was an empty lot.

"This auction is in less than two weeks," Graham said. On the drive home, his data mind produced a litany of reasons why I couldn't run a garden center there. Just as with that person who doubted my ability to sell my house, I looked at him and said, "Watch me," as lovingly as I could.

In the two weeks following and through the wizardry of Google maps, we "toured" urban garden centers all across the United States. We gathered data to end all data about garden centers, but for Graham, it was never enough. I tried to stay strong for the two of us as we proceeded. Though confident with Graham in the car that night, I was completely undecided as to whether this was the path for me. After years of searching, failed job attempts, part-time work, and saying no to corporate life, I was met with indecision.

As I debated, I had both dreams and nightmares about the property I was considering buying. It had a metal building of about 1000 square feet, a small area for a parking lot, and a chain link fence surrounding the entire property. It was utilitarian at best, but also perfect for a little garden center. The pie-shaped prop-

erty sat along Market Street, a major road in Chattanooga. It stretched from 19th Street almost to 20[th,] where
a different owner stored cars on the corner of the same
block. The entrance was at the corner of 19th and Market
streets. Across the street were three boarded-up commer-
cial buildings. Next door was a vacant lot. On the next
block up Market was a barbeque joint and a hair salon.
An industrial recycling company had rehabilitated the
building next to theirs and planted magnolia trees and
decorative grasses. Four blocks up was a school and the
Chattanooga Choo Choo from the famous song of the
same name. Main Street, with restaurants and art galler-
ies lining both sides, was also four blocks away. Chattanooga was brimming with development, but not in that
location yet. Depending on the hour, I thought it was a
pile of potential or a foolish risk.

It is rare that a business plan begins with Step 1: Go
to an auction. Step 2: Win the auction. There was no way
to predict that my bidding amount was larger than the
other bidders. Had we considered other properties? No.
This one was the one. It was just right in so many ways.
I neither had my heart set on it, nor could let the idea go
for fear of losing.

The night before the auction, I went to dinner with
my new Chattanooga friend, Barb. I drove her home and
told her about my indecisiveness. "Do you want to pray
about it?" she asked. Despite going to church for years
in DC and being a Christian, I wasn't comfortable at all
with praying together, particularly about business. But
here I was in the South, and I'd heard that they did that

sort of thing here. We commenced praying. After that, I went home and got a good night's sleep. A greater force was listening. I had given my power there.

On the car ride to the auction, Graham and I reviewed our numbers and bidding strategy. He is a calm and gentle man and was an ideal bidder. He is also really good with numbers and, frankly, a better listener, which comes in handy at an auction. Off we went.

In the car, I thought about my mom. I prayed that she was looking over us—and approved. The money from the wrongful death case after she died from complications of her accident was partially paying for this venture. I wanted to do right by her and honor her beautifully.

I was the only woman at the auction. Though Graham was doing the bidding, it was clear that I was the interested party. The words flew by and, as auctioneers do, it went very fast. A few bidders dropped off together in a clump. That left a few of us for the remainder. Then there were two. I had a feeling the other had the same top number I did and told Graham to go $5,000 higher. We won! We gave our deposit and planned details with the brokers. My life changed in that moment.

Though it was 11 a.m. and I am not generally a morning drinker, I wanted a beer quickly. It was shocking to spend that amount of money that fast. It was also shocking to begin this enterprise. A few minutes later, we sat at a restaurant with a pint of ice cold IPA in front of us. I could hear my mom cheering. Maybe I was channeling her. She was a flamboyant and gleeful celebrant and loved her martinis.

Mom on an evening of martinis

The biggest lesson I got was this: my prayers were answered. For years, I'd prayed for work that put my mixed bag of skills to use. I prayed to be used up in worthy work. This was it. Delivering workshops and one-on-one consults would stretch my education wings. Botanically-themed items for the home would put my interior design degree and years in architecture firms to good use. Social media, promotional events, public speaking, and market strategy gave my marketing know-how room to grow. Inventory management, hiring, financial planning, and facility management would test my business experience. The retail environment would tap into my sales experience. Best of all, as a life-long gardener whose favorite job yet was flinging plants around with college kids, I had a home of my own to do just that.

This was a huge lesson in giving up control, especially

given the unpredictability of an auction. In a way, I ceded control at this moment. I felt peace, and I felt that it was going to be alright. I realized, as I had in the field with the horses, that I was a tiny part in a giant Universe that all worked as one.

CHAPTER SEVEN:

Bees' Beginnings, Our Beginnings

Everyone wants to ride with you in the limo,
but what you want is someone who will take
the bus with you when the limo breaks down.

—Oprah Winfrey

The first thing I got for our new garden center was the biggest dumpster I could find. Graham set to work adding a bounty of unwanted items into it. A 1970s glass desk that looked like it came out of a disco, went off to Habitat for Humanity. Mauve, the trendy color from the early 1980s, covered walls of plastic laminate slot board often used in dime stores and gas stations. Rusty metal lights, hung from chains, went to the dumpster next. The walls were covered in plastic panels, vines that had creeped in from outside, and bugs—all good dumpster candidates. The floor was caked with mud, chewing gum wads, wax, and the remains from the meat market that was once there. The walls and space in front of a walk-in freezer were similarly coated in grime. Outside, overgrown shrubs and trees poked into the space where cars should drive. Monster-sized, ten-foot rose bushes with thorns built for battle offered a sickly flower or two, covered in fungus. Into the dumpster they went.

For display, we turned to Craigslist and Habitat stores to buy tables and shelving units. Unlike when I was selling inherited items in Virginia on Craigslist, this time I was on the buying side. I scoured the listings for styles that would fit together once in one large space. Old, round oak tables with a center base were paired with industrial-style shelves and formal sofa tables. With paint, they'd all have a cohesive look. We gathered supplies to update our new treasures. Our assembly line process went like this: I'd contact the buyer and get the address, Graham would go get a table, then our first intern Bryanna and I—and later, a new friend, Shelli—would paint them in the parking lot. In about the time it took to paint one table, Graham would return with another one, and we'd paint that one too.

Meanwhile, we were getting the walls to reflect a new style. We found an amazing woman-owned hardwood mill a few blocks away. They used lumber from local trees being cut down because of home additions needing room, storms, and other development. We selected some poplar with lovely light orange and purple tones. A light whitewash stain was mixed to unify and seal these pretty colors. A second intern rubbed stain into the boards on sawhorses in the parking lot. Drivers honked their horn as they went by; nothing had been in that spot for years. Licensed contractors did all the heavy lifting, but if allowed by City rules and inspections, we did as much ourselves as we possibly could.

After getting a bid for over $3,000 to do the floors, Graham and I decided to do them ourselves. The city didn't require us to use licensed contractors for this task, so off we went to Home Depot for supplies after watching hours of YouTube videos on how to do the work. Next, we peeled buckets of gum, wax, and who knows what else off the floors. Then we used a machine to scrub and scour them, and mopped them with industrial cleanser. After 40 five-gallon buckets of dirty water were hauled out of there, I sat down in a puddle and cried. My back hurt, and I was just done with mops and buckets. I declared the floor clean and said whatever got sealed in there was the cleanest dirt in Chattanooga. We went out to dinner and returned the next day to seal the clean dirt with a stain and a glossy finish. It looked just like the pictures on Pinterest and saved us about $2,700.

That left one other big elephant of a refrigerator to remove. Environmental codes and standards prevented us from disposing of it. Refurbishing companies had plenty of old ones and didn't want ours. After weeks of ads in the paper and various online publications, we were still stuck with the 12' x 15' monster. We began asking friends in the restaurant business to spread the word. Soon we got a call from a sandwich shop in Georgia willing to remove it and put it to use. We thanked our lucky stars . . . and now have a lifetime supply of hoagies waiting for us in Georgia as repayment!

MilA HANSFORD

Cath and Graham in front of the refrigerator
about to be removed.

Graham generally stayed on site to manage the activity while Bryanna, our intern, and I would be back at our house, researching vendors, placing orders, and finding

sources for bags, tissue, stickers, and a host of other supplies. A graphic designer worked on signage, chic square
brochures, and more.

The designer and I worked on color schemes and the
overall look, but she needed a name to create a logo. Soon
after, I was on the phone with Michelle discussing this
conundrum. In my past, I'd worked on various naming
systems and brands, and knew that naming is an important matter. It needs to be catchy, memorable, have a good
story, and say something about the business. The exception these days are tech companies—Lord knows what
half those company names mean. Then there was the
expected: green, plant, Cath's Garden Center, and such.
I didn't want to be limited and defined as just a garden
center, anyway. I was stuck.

I called my friend Michelle to brainstorm. As usual,
Michelle and I had two conversations going: one about
the business name and another about murals I'd photo-
graphed to entertain myself while living in Richmond,
Virginia. Of the 350 murals I'd documented, my and
Graham's favorite was of bees on unicycles painted by
artist Matt Lively. I mashed up the two and said, "This
business wouldn't be like one bee on one unicycle, though.
It would be lots of bees riding one bike, working together.
You know, like bees on a bicycle."

We stopped. Ah, the alliteration and playfulness of
that. The presence of pollinators and environmental reference to cycling was cool too. I knew I had a winner. I
quickly got off the phone and bought the web address,
signed up for the Facebook and Instagram names, and

got the Gmail address for good measure. Soon, Graham got busy registering the name at all the proper authorities. It was real: Bees on a Bicycle (we fondly call it Bees) was a true business entity!

Now that we were real with a name and all, it was time to think about how best to accomplish things. If you are a fan of business publications, you may have noticed an admiration for hiring people that have experienced failure in some form. With several previous business ventures, I had experienced plenty of failure mixed in with success. I paired that with my favorite quote about money: "It's not the money you make, but what you don't spend." It makes so much sense to me, particularly after my thriftiness schooling from Graham.

I knew from experience that two major business expenses are facility and staff. I'd solved the facility thing by winning my property at auction. Already my property taxes and fees, divided by 12 months in a year, was lower than rents in the area. Rents would increase in time, and that number would only get better. That left staff. As a startup, I knew the longer I could hold off on getting full-time employees, the better. What I had was time and teaching experience, and I planned to put it to use. I reached out to the local university about interns. They, in turn, interviewed me for two hours about my internship program. As a former teacher, I prepared a robust entrepreneurship and business skills lesson plan, to be tailored for each student placed at Bees.

The internship program has grown, from one thankfully perfect applicant our first semester, to over 20 interested candidates just over a year later. One thing all interns have had in common is that they've all had what Mom used to call "a good cry" at Bees. As a professional who typically worked in an office, it's been unusual (unless it was me) for me to see crying. These interns have all let loose for a range of reasons including no-shows at parties, roommate issues, boyfriends calling it quits, and parental wrongdoings. What I wasn't paying in salary was certainly stretching my parental wings! I did my best to soothe tired and worried minds. What I loved is that I'd created a work environment where expressing emotion was OK, where I was a trusted advisor for advice, and where I could lend a shoulder when no words were necessary. For someone who was a stepmom of two and had only limited deep friendships a few years previously, this was a whole new world. There have been days I drove home from work and marveled at the difference. I treasure a text from our intern Madison: "I am so proud of you and your ability to run Bees. It has been such a blessing to be a part of your business. You are one of the hardest workers I know, and I am grateful for the skills that you passed down to me."

Brennan was our intern our first Spring that Bees was open, and she learned right alongside me. We had a rocky start and disagreed on things with stern looks and opinions. I persevered, though, and focused on what she could benefit from as a business major. We gained each other's' trust, and soon she came to me for advice for a whole array of life and school issues.

What we had together was more than an intern/boss

Brennan and Cath

relationship, like sisters or a niece and trusted aunt. When it came time to go at the end of the semester, she and I were both teary. I wanted to give her a present, but knew that wasn't really appropriate for a boss to do. We talked about it, and I thought she was going to break down from crying so hard. Wrapped in tissue was a necklace from my mom. The inscription said, "Reach for the stars. If you miss, shoot for the moon." Evidently that phrase was one she had used throughout life as a mantra. It reached her and was the perfect gift. She and I parted ways, and I am forever changed by her strong will and eventual willingness to learn and contribute.

When customers came to Bees once it opened, my listening ear and sympathetic way came in handy. Customers would often come to Bees to honor a loved one who had passed, to buy a gift for themselves after a fight or a job loss, or to soothe a hard choice. It was important to know when and how to listen in these important interactions. The interns prepared me for that in their own way.

Two weeks before opening, we were in dire need of a website. We had been sharing our daily story on Facebook and Instagram, but there was not one single place to find out about the business. I chose a website-building platform and began work. As the site began to take form, I thought of how just a few years before I'd have sold a similar site at our agency in DC for thousands of dollars! How just a few years of technological development had changed things. In that I had been involved in several hundred sites at our agency, I drew upon that experience. The writing drew upon my stint in corporate communications, as did the daily social media posts. That alone could have been a full-time job. But in addition, I was researching vendors, gathering plants, doing merchandising, settling last-minute construction details, and selecting things like cash registers, shopping bag sizes, ceiling fans, doorknobs, and paint colors. It was a dizzying array of tasks to complete and gather together for opening day.

About a month before our launch, I woke up and considered my various construction garb options. I wanted to throw on my usual paint-splattered t-shirt, but had a strong sense, in the back of my mind, not to do that. Instead, I picked a trusty black sundress that looks sharp on me, and off I went to Bees to see construction progress and meet with vendors. Lumber and half-done projects were everywhere. It must have been interesting because one of the lead writers from *The Chattanooga News Press*, our local newspaper, stopped and asked for an interview. I've been interviewed by journalists before, but never saw someone take notes with one hand and photos with the other. I would be mid-sentence and bam! a photo would be taken. I had images of me in a weird position with a grimace on my face being in the newspaper. This journalist knew what he was doing, thankfully. The next day, there was a nice-looking, six-inch shot of me on the front page of the business section. Thank God I'd listened to my Spidey-sense and worn something presentable!

A week before opening, we were busily building plant stands and gathering plants from various growers. I drove out to one in the middle of Tennessee woods, my handy GPS on my phone guiding the way through a list of left and right turns. After hours of selecting and packing plants, I prepared to head back. My phone was useless, gathering absolutely no data in those woods. The directions from the vendor weren't helpful either in that there weren't street names or postal route numbers posted. I had a printed map of Tennessee and a rear-view mirror compass showing whether I was going east, west, north or south. Oh, joy. From the map, I saw that the major highway was about an inch north from where I was. I weaved my way left and right, always choosing north. I got to the highway eventually and had used almost all my gas doing it. My grit and determination were tested that day.

After writing the umpteenth check for contractors, supplies, inventory, and all else, I stumbled onto one of the most effective and far-reaching marketing techniques I've ever executed. It began by me refusing to buy the cardboard boxes with low sides that garden centers give customers to use for plant purchases. The prices were ridiculous—and did we really need more boxes in our environment, anyway? I was petulant and tired. I decided to get on NextDoor, a neighborhood app, to see if anyone had any boxes from mail-order companies lying around. To this day, we haven't had to pay for boxes, and the people bringing them have often turned into customers. They are thrilled to see their online habits helping a small business. What I didn't know at the time was that this would be the first of many environmental decisions to become a cornerstone of the Bees on a Bicycle brand. Our motto, "Foster community; create beauty," flowed out of this experience.

Reusing boxes was our somewhat unplanned entry into community involvement. As we developed as a company, initiatives like the boxes, the intern program, and our involvement with various philanthropic efforts as well as pollinator awareness and educational programming became key facets of our community focus—as well as the worldwide community at large. As I learned about products, I learned more about how truly un-environmental gardening is. A hobby of millions of Americans, gardening is laden with chemicals in the form of pesticides, fertilizers, and plastic pots. As we gardened using these methods—I had been using these unsound practices myself for many years—I learned that we are hurting the environment more than helping it.

Three of many within the Bees community

I asked myself: if I were truly going to create beauty and foster community, what would be a responsible way to address these issues and address them with integrity? I sat down and began reading. I attended seminars and talked to experts. I interviewed growers and consulted lists and sets of recommendations. I sifted through much of what the USDA was saying carefully—it was laden with chemical company lobbying efforts through and through.

Given that our company was called Bees on a Bicycle, I took time to learn about bees and other pollinators, the challenges they are facing, their decline in numbers, and the relation of them to our food supply for humans. This led to learning about invasive plants, fertilizer effects on our water supply, particularly the Tennessee River, and neonicotinoid pesticides as well. I was learning, and my customers along with me, that the environment belongs to all of us. I truly believe it is our collective responsibility. For example, I learned that 85 percent of United States land is privately owned. If we are to create habitable homes for the declining pollinators that in turn pollinate our food supply, we as private land owners need to step up and do something. It is a true community (i.e., not government) effort. Gardening, at least where Bees on a Bicycle was concerned, was taking on a bigger and bigger message and role every day.

There were days that this new information, my perceived role to disseminate it, and my responsibility as a new business owner put a weight on me that was unfun. Why couldn't I just sell blingy and bright, filled with fertilizer plants like the next guy? For good reasons. It was a way for our company to differentiate us from competitors and offer something unique. Second, it was the right thing to do. People were responding to it, but needed education and encouragement. This meant Bees would be selling plants in a whole different way than the typical garden center. This endeavor took every ounce of what I'd learned when I got my master's in education! Yet another way Bees was using my assortment of oddball experiences.

When Fred and I would go for walks, I'd think about how quickly things were flowing for Bees. I'd been involved with many other companies before and had only seen this sort of flow with the AIDS Memorial Quilt. Things just happened for that Quilt like they were scripted. It was amazing—and so it was with Bees. One thing flowed into the next. Mind you, it wasn't a cake walk, and there were many roadblocks. What I noticed, though, was a sense of movement and choreography of events unlike I'd seen when I owned other businesses. All this movement and flow involved incredibly hard work, but as needs arose, they were answered.

You'd think that once I discovered this ask-and-answer flow thing that I'd rub the genie bottle often. It was almost the opposite. I found myself being almost afraid of what the Universe had in store for me. Things were moving along at a fair clip, but when it came to asking God (I believe in God, but you may call a higher power something else) for what I needed, I was either clueless about what I needed, didn't want to ask (i.e., I felt unworthy), or was just confused and swimming as fast as I could. This combination of bumbling and awareness helped keep things going at a fair pace!

As Graham managed the construction, he must have been thinking about life and those beyond himself too. Graham is generally a quiet guy, but every once in a while, he talks about what is on his mind in a simple, eloquent way. When he does this, it is obvious he has given his words and thoughts a great deal of time and attention.

One day, Graham came home from the construction site with cobwebs in his hair and dirt covering the rest of him. He talked about family, life, where we were heading, and what he saw in me. He talked about me in his life and how he wanted me in his life forever. We'd been together eight years, but after he'd bought our house for us to live in, we'd talked about marriage too. As the data-gatherer, he continued to ponder, and that day (or possibly long before), he'd been thinking. On he went some more about love and how proud of me he was. He talked about what I was for him and how we complimented each other. "Are you proposing?" I asked. He dropped to his knee and asked me to marry him. I was filled with gratitude. I hugged my dusty and cobwebby guy and adored him so fully that moment.

There is asking the Universe for what you want, and then there is asking the city office that gives occupancy permits for what you want. We bought the property February 24th, and met with the city planning department that granted permits soon after. We were moving one wall and adding an interior door. In that we were a garden center, we asked that the permit be granted in the spring, preferably late winter. No go. It looked like we'd open in the heat of the summer, well after the busy spring planting season. In the building inspection department's defense, Chattanooga is growing at a rapid rate and they were scrambling to keep up with the permits and reviews to make buildings safe. This was especially brought to our attention when one of the antique brick buildings fell into a heap further down Market Street. Inspections like ours weren't in effect when that building was built or renovated. They certainly made sense, though, after seeing the pile of rubble! Luckily, no one was hurt.

The first day of summer, June 21st, Bees on a Bicycle was approved to open. If you have been in Tennessee in the summer or attended Bonnaroo, a music festival up the road around that time, it is a combination of hot and humid like you would not believe. Add a bunch of pavement to the mix, and the temperature soars.

But a summer opening was the card we drew, and we had to play our hand. As the months rolled on and we were learning all things garden center, I thanked my lucky stars we didn't open in the spring. We could have done it, but I'd have been working beyond-insane hours. I preferred just plain ol' insane hours for the first year!

As the year wore on, we needed to get realistic about Graham working at Bees. For a mathematician, it wasn't a good match. Despite our love for each other and our ability to divide tasks efficiently for the opening, we weren't ideal workmates. We needed separate workplaces, and, frankly, separate incomes for our household expenses.

For months, I'd been driving across the Tennessee River and pointing at a large insurance company building. "That's where Graham will work when the time is right!" I'd say. A few weeks after he began his job search, he applied for a job there and was hired. I have to admit I get envious about job searches for Graham. He barely says the word "work," and he gets hired. He is so darn smart, is an incredibly likeable and easy-going fellow, and his skills are in such high demand. Unlike yours truly, he is the yin to my yang when it comes to finding work! What it did begin, though, was a realization of how much what I said and asked for was being answered. I had prayed before the auction, and we got the property. I had needed help, and the university had responded with a great program for interns. I had refused to buy boxes, and the community had provided. I had pointed and declared at a building, and Graham had begun to work there. What else was in store for me? Ironically, I was afraid to ask or even imagine. I just put my head down and worked hard for many months.

Graham's employment left me alone at Bees, minus the hustle and bustle of vendors preparing for opening and an intern filling in the gaps. From time to time, it would get lonely in between customers. In the winter, it got dreadfully cold and damp too. Like the interns before me, I sat down one day and had a good cry. Even if a business is bustling and ideal, there are moments when you question your sanity. I was bone tired, cold, and damp. For good measure, I'd just broken up the ice for the umpteenth time in the demonstration garden so the fish would have a little breathing room. Needless to say, no one was buying plants. To add to my temporary despair, it was sleeting.

The door chimes rang, and I dried my eyes on my sleeve. "This should be good," I thought sarcastically. I was a mess.

Maddie entered like a ray of sunshine in the middle of a wintery, dark, sleeting storm. She introduced herself as a student at a nearby college, a photo enthusiast, and someone who had been following us online. She was thrilled about the store, what she saw us doing, and what she'd read about us. She was fascinated by me and set to learn more with a series of intense questions. I did my best to answer her heartfelt inquiries with dry eyes, but it was no use. I sat there and wept in front of this young customer. Someone who cared deeply, was enthusiastic, and really understood what I was doing with Bees. She arrived on our doorstep at the perfect time. "Who are you?" I asked. "You coming here today is like being visited by an angel."

We talked for an hour, something that has been repeated many times with other customers, many of whom encouraged me to write this book. But Maddie was the first on that wet and dark day. She asked, in the Southern tradition, "May I pray for you?" I let her. I was open to whatever she had for me. Her wisdom reached beyond her years. Since that time, she visited Bees a few times and even prayed for an intern who was going through a tough time herself. We stay in touch on Instagram, forged in a lifelong bond from that touching moment that cold February day.

The visit with Maddie wasn't the darkest day that year. That day began with a poop. Fred had come to work with me and was fascinated with something on the sidewalk as I fumbled with my keys for the gate. I looked down and gave a stern, "No-no, Fred!' He was snout distance away from a large pile of human feces. I went inside our building and weighed my options. I decided to call Graham. In his data analyst, loving way he asked, "How do you know it is human poop?"

"Because I've been pooping for over 50 years and picking up dog poop since 1996," I replied. This analysis wasn't making the situation better.

I got off the phone and did what any sane business owner would do: I sat down and cried. Then I called Michelle. "What's going on?" she asked through my sobs.

I was ready for a good cry and wasn't letting up. "Someone shit on my business!"

"What do you mean?" she asked.

I explained the situation. The thought of someone either angry, drunk, or homeless and in need of a proper facility swirled in my head. It was all too much. She and I weighed the possibilities, talked about how lousy the economic situation was getting for many poor souls here in the US, and I fortified myself for sidewalk cleaning.

Off I went, plastic bag in hand. As have many others, I'd changed diapers and dealt with bathroom needs of aging parents. This was different. There was an indignance in my emotions and also a supreme sadness about what society had come to and what this neighborhood had become. Since our motto is "Foster community; create beauty," that day I felt I was fighting an uphill battle in the beauty part. The fact that I'd collected an entire bag of litter the day before added to my sadness. I took the proverbial deep breath (but not a literal one) and picked up the poop. There is nothing like picking up poop to make one realize that they are but a small part of a much bigger picture.

As we were open longer, we began to have repeat customers. One set of customers was like Maddie, but more my age. I came to call them the Zen Waterers. In their role at Bees, they rarely watered, but the term referred to the washing of our space in generosity and kindness. It also was an opportunity for peace, joy, and much else for the people who came to us wanting to lend a hand.

"I could just come in here and shop all the time, or I could help you," Pat noticed. "I love being here and want to help what you're doing. This is my happy place, and I need a reason to return frequently other than shopping."

I needed help beyond interns at that point, and that piqued my interest. I could always use customers, but hey, help was good too. Soon, Pat and Mary Lou came as needed off and on to ease my load. They were joined by Shelli, Lindsey, Marcelle, and Steph for special occasions.

This was particularly helpful the weekend Graham and I got married. I didn't want to be the kind of shop that closed for personal reasons, but Bees' sole employee was getting married on a Saturday, the number one day of the week in retail. The Zen Waterers plus current and past interns came to the rescue in two-hour shifts, keeping the store open.

My intern at wedding time was Madison. About three weeks before the wedding, she came into Bees and announced, "Today we are working on your wedding!" She was getting nervous and justifiably so. Ten days before the wedding day, we had the ribbon cutting for Bees on a Bicycle! Call us crazy, but it made sense to get all the activity and hoopla grouped into one month. We had geared up for that with a big PR push, and a mountain of customers and visitors showed up to welcome Bees to the community. At the official ribbon cutting, a group of 40 or 50 well-wishers gathered in front of Bees for a photo. I held a giant pair of scissors and cut the ribbon.

We ate and drank well that afternoon, celebrating a business underway and growing.

STEPHANIE EVERETT

Cutting the ribbon.

Somehow, amongst the ribbon cutting, my learning curve about running a garden center, and fall planting season, the wedding hadn't gotten the attention it needed. The catering hadn't been confirmed, Graham hadn't bought a suit yet, and we had no idea about which flowers to choose, what music made sense for the ceremony, or transportation to the reception.

Other key details were missing too. Yes, it was both Graham's and my second wedding, but no, we didn't want it to be silly or disorganized. We did have the invites out, and all but two guests had replied that they were descending on Chattanooga for our happy day. Per her announcement, Madison and I set to work on the wedding immediately. I will be forever grateful for her putting down her foot! The guests were fed, drank well, gazed upon flowers, and listened to music, thanks to our efforts ten days before the wedding occurred.

The week before the wedding, Graham and I went to the local flower wholesalers to see what was in season. We also arranged for a local flower farmer to supplement our botanical bounty. A day before, Marcia and I created bouquets for the church and house in record time. Long ago, as fellow cattle-rustlers in our animal communications course in Arizona, we had learned to work effectively as a team. Marcia is an avid gardener and was perfect for the job. The day of our wedding, our nieces, nephews, kids, and their mates gathered to create bridesmaid, bride, and groom boutonnieres and more. The front porch of our house turned into a temporary florist shop as Pinterest photos were used as inspiration. It all pulled together beautifully. The colors of the late-autumn season were lush and deep. Goldenrod, asters, amaranth, globe thistle, dahlias, and chrysanthemums were wrapped in bountiful greenery, herbs, and deep-colored ribbons. The blooms were full and fun to carry and arrange. We made something beautiful that perfectly warm and clear autumn day.

My friends with a capital F gathered at the back of the church with me: Lise, Michelle, Michele, Marcia, and Jayne. Gigi was unable to join us, but was there in spirit. They wore midnight blue dresses they'd insisted on wearing. I had wanted them to wear whatever they pleased, but they wanted to be more of a posse and connected to me—I was touched and incredibly honored. The flowers my new family had arranged looked amazing against their deeply colored dresses. Prior to the ceremony, a set of rock, reggae, and jazz songs that reminded Graham and me of love played on the church sound system. A rotating set of 20 slides with both of us from the past eight years together showed on two screens. The bouquets Marcia and I had created were positioned at the front of the church. One bouquet was so large that Marcia's husband Steve used 15 gallons of water to fill the vase.

Standing in the back awaiting the procession music, my self-proclaimed posse of dear friends sang *Stand by Me* to me as Keith Walker, later to sing in Carnegie Hall, belted out the words to the guests attending. Each of my bridesmaids then walked down the aisle alone. Jayne, my maid of honor, squeezed my hand and went last before me. I thought about her, years ago, packing my kitchen. Then it was my turn to go, also walking alone. Both Mom and Dad had died, and I had no siblings, or uncles, so there I was, escorting myself. I was at peace with that, but emotional about the step I was taking. Gratitude filled me, as well as happiness, anticipation, and relief. I was a mess. I didn't cry, but I was very moved and my face showed it. I stopped halfway down the aisle. Graham came down off the stage to greet me and escorted me the rest of the way.

Foster community; create beauty. A new community surrounded us. It pulled together, and a wedding and ribbon-cutting ceremony came together beautifully.

One would think that chicken bones would be no big deal after such feats. Nope! Nothing illustrates community spirit and ingenuity like what I call the "chicken bone caper."

Bees sits next to a bus stop where people often eat a bit of chicken from the corner gas station before they catch the bus. One day, poof! The public waste can was removed. After which, on Saturdays, I'd begin my day by picking up chicken bones thrown over the fence into Bees, among other trash, bottles, and all else. Graham noticed the city workers dodging traffic and picking up the rest off of Market Street and made friends with them in our chicken bone plight. The city workers assured us the trash can had been requested and would come back soon. Months of trash collection ensued. Not my ideal way to start the day at all! The city workers were tired of trash collection in the traffic too.

Finally, we public and private trash collectors had a tete-a-tete. I, as a business owner and citizen, would make a request. After an hour of being passed around via phone, I spoke to the person whose office is in the place where they fix the city busses. He had jurisdiction over the trash cans at the bus stops too. It was decided that the bus company would place a trash can at the stop, but the city would be responsible for emptying it. Whatever the combo, I wanted fewer chicken bones to pick up. A few days later, a trash can was installed and the trash on Market Street was reduced almost entirely. As Hillary Clinton famously said: "It takes a village."

CHAPTER EIGHT:

Bees Blooms

A wise man once told me luck isn't
some mystical energy that dances around the Universe
randomly bestowing people with satisfaction
and joy, you create your own luck.

—Jay-Z

When someone wished me luck, it made me think one of two things. The first is that they had no idea about entrepreneurial success. It comes from patience, persistence, and grit. This success uses a bounty of skills behind it such as organization, accounting, marketing, finance, facility management, and operations. The ability to work with others (vendors, customers, government inspectors, millennial interns, etc.), lies at the foundation of success. Luck? Not so much. Faith? Yes. Perspective from faith and skill? Yes.

There is a second thing I thought about with luck wishers. It happens less and less these days, but when Bees was new and people were figuring out what we provided, sometimes that didn't meet their needs. That is to be expected; you can't be all things to all people. At times though, when needs weren't met and perceived time and effort were wasted by the customer, I'd get a hair flip and an eye roll and a "Good luck!" as they sauntered out the door. In other words, "You're screwed! You aren't meeting my [or anyone else's] needs at all, and I had to get out of my car and everything!"

I used to get upset about this. Now I lump them in with the other luck-wishers. They just don't know what to say and are doing their best. I reply with a thank you and move on with the people who know and love what Bees on a Bicycle does. Thankfully, that circle of people is growing daily.

In some ways, these luck-wishers may have been hinting at the art of patience. Unlike restaurants or movies that open with a bang, retail is known to grow over time. Provided, some well-heeled brands are eagerly awaited and hit pay dirt from the start in new locations, but new brands, particularly those that deliver unexpected product lines, take time and patience. Bees fits in that latter category.

One could posit that a gal who waited eight years for a man to ask her to marry her has loads of patience. I do not. I was ready to cart Graham off to the church way before he came home with his sweaty and lovely proposal. Patience was not one of my virtues. I'm working on it though, dammit! So how do I keep myself from watching the water boil, per se? I hone crafts. Writing was one of such crafts. I see what I can do in 100 words or less in a social media post. I tried different writing angles and directions learned from *The Elements of Style* by Strunk and White . . . I wrote a book.

Instagram was an incredibly useful exercise during this time. The average Instagram user is 30 years younger than me, so it was a bit of an adjustment to learn the style, common language used there, and etiquette. Yes, there is Instagram etiquette. For example, unlike Facebook, it is rare for someone to really spout off about a topic. Instagram is largely a visual platform, and thus comments are kept light and short, generally.

I decided the day we won the property auction that I'd post on Instagram and Facebook at least once a day for the first year. By the time we had our ribbon-cutting ceremony five months later, we had over a thousand followers, not all of them in Chattanooga. We have regular fans and commenters as far away as Australia. This multi-continent aspect of Bees on a Bicycle's daily life is our connection to a global community—especially with posts about pollinators, our food supply with their involvement, and other environmental issues. The concept of "we are of one Universe" was never so present to me as when on Instagram.

As a result of my (almost) daily Instagram posts and my comments on others' activities, I met key influencers in Chattanooga, potential customers, unique vendors, sources of inspiration, other businesses similar to mine, businesses facing similar challenges, and more. It was and will be a treasure trove of information and usefulness. Posts varied from education about gardening, behind the scenes views of challenges, humor, stories about Fred, philosophy, inspiration, product shots, poetry, Shakespearian quotes, references to game shows, kid memories, and more. Generally, I tried to keep the posts light and offer an online sanctuary to match the oasis we endeavored to provide in person at our shop.

One day, a 70-mile-per-hour car crash occurred just feet from our front door. It was shocking and dangerous, and shook me in that I was just feet away. I debated whether to break the tradition of sanctuary with a post about danger, death, and irresponsible driving. I took a deep breath, took a photo of the crash site, and posted my views. A few days later, a customer came to the shop specifically because of that post. "I had to see what this shop was after reading that," she said. Parents from the school a few blocks away thanked me. A teacher has since reached out to direct grant money to Bees for their garden area plants. When something less than pleasant involved community, I made an exception.

These community posts soon took a positive turn, complete with a customer taking the lead to do fundraising to help an animal-related effort. Skip, who manages the car wash a few doors down 19th Street, takes care of the feral cats in our neighborhood. I'd been talking with him about trap, neuter, and release (TNR). In animal welfare groups, this is the top way to help these little kitties, complete with vaccinations, to lead healthier lives. At that point, I was involved with a few other neighborhood concerns (illegal dumping, storm water management, educating kids on environmental issues, pollinator awareness, speeding on Market Street) and asked the heavens to send me help on this one. "Skip, you're going to have 300 cats soon," was all I could offer. That and a request to the Universe. Well, a few weeks later, a staff person and a volunteer from Chattanooga's animal welfare facility came to Bees to shop. I introduced them to Skip so they could address the situation. Go neighborhood TNR love for those cats! Foster community. After posting on Instagram about this turn of events, neighbors volunteered donations to the effort.

So one could say that Instagram was a platform for Bees on a Bicycle to foster community. My posts were different than what was popular though, which took a bit of courage. They were noticed and gained loyal following, particularly the heartfelt and vulnerable ones. This wasn't expected or planned.

When I began posting on Instagram, the term, "Instagram pink" was a well-known visual filter often used by many brands. Plants in dark, almost black soil aren't Instagram pink. The floor where I photographed many of our products was a dark grey. A dark and rich color scheme for Bees on a Bicycle soon developed. In the interest of time and with no other options, really, when it came to soil color, I stuck with my dark green, Aegean blue, and dark neutral colors. Interestingly, dark and moody became the hot photographic trend six months later. If anything, I'd learned to say what you needed to say visually and otherwise and stick to it!

After a few months of posts, I was asked to teach a class about Instagram with additional class requests since. How ironic that I'd actually be teaching this after not getting job after job in communications using social media, among other tools. I prepared my talk and showed up. In the room were approximately 25 millennials and a few folks my age hoping to learn what I'd gathered in a few months (plus 13 years at our agency in the background). I did a little happy dance for a moment and did my best to appear like an expert.

Besides Instagram, the entire botanical kingdom beckoned and needed understanding. There was a mountain of data to learn. In that I was learning things to bide my time and garner patience, this one could take a lifetime. From time to time, clients asked about a plant that's green, has leaves, and grows. You know the one. The plant. Oh yes, that one. "The plant kingdom is large," I explained, and we left it at that. As for me and this Universe of green, I am challenged by an endless array of things to learn. For example: botanical terminology; plants that grow well in urban settings, containers, the state of Tennessee, humidity, high wind, and a host of other environmental factors; blooming seasons; native vs cultivar vs ornamental, and a bunch of other topics.

An ongoing and significant sub-topic is environmental and earth-savvy gardening practices. When I was slinging plants in the garden center in Richmond, I noticed that there was almost as much square footage devoted to herbicides and pesticides as there was for plants. When I helped customers in that area, the rims of my eyes would burn. I assumed that was from the chemicals, but as I mentioned earlier, I am sensitive to all sorts of things. But the question begged for attention: were those of us who were sensitive to these products like canaries in a coal mine, indicating future danger for the rest of the population? Were bees dying in massive numbers offering a similar warning beacon?

As the owner of a company called Bees on a Bicycle, I owed it to all bees to make informed environmental choices. I decided not to carry fertilizers, herbicides, or pesticides, even though the sale of these items is incredibly profitable. There was gardening and food production long before these bags of pellets came around. The challenge for our company was to bring chemical-free gardening to people in such a way to be informative and not preachy, elegant yet not excessive, comprehensive yet entertaining. The challenge for me as a business woman was to fashion a product line that could survive without the income from sales of bags of chemicals and the plants that needed them routinely.

I continued to find other ways that gardening can improve environmentally. For example, plants came from the grower in plastic pots. Meanwhile, plastic is filling our landfills and oceans at exponential rates. I decided not to sell plastic pots to provide a Bees'-sized counterbalance. It was a start. Tiny, but mighty, right? As a small retailer, I had little or no sway over the growers and the plastic pots they chose.

To add to our box re-use community efforts, we found a plastic pot alternative to offer customers. These pots are made of grain fiber. They are lightweight, come in great colors, and have the feel of plastic (but fibery and better!). When we announced the change, it became one of our most interacted-with posts on social media— people were fascinated to put a by-product of the food industry to good use.

These grain fiber pots range from small to pumpkin-sized, and I was thrilled with them, but then I started thinking about the big pots people put on their porches and in front of businesses. This was an even bigger way to not use plastic! In addition to the environmental aspects, I considered first impressions, branding and how gardens at our doorways are a window to our beliefs. I also worried that I was reading too much into a pot, drank massive amounts of coffee, and paced around the house.

After my coffee-induced big-think, I sat down to write a manifesto, of sorts. I wrote about how we can do better than surround our homes with plastic, how we can actually save money by purchasing quality, one-of-a-kind pottery and have something to treasure. It mattered to me that people break the cheap/disposable/landfill cycle of large-pot purchases. It also mattered to me that they have handsome choices at decent prices for planters in this town. This became my first blog post, one that would in turn necessitate a new and improved web site. There needed to be a platform where I could display bigger ideas in more words than spiffy Instagram posts. I was finding that other people were thinking some of the same thoughts too. Some even enjoyed what I had to say. Others self-selected and shopped elsewhere. That's OK. Not all of us were meant to shop at the same place.

And where were people currently going to get large planters? Big box stores. Off I went to a few big box stores to do research and see how we can differentiate ourselves. What I found is that they not only had very limited selection and options—beige, clay-colored, and black, all shaped the same way—but were often more expensive than what Bees was carrying!

This experience and research folded into another set of new beliefs on shopping small and buying locally. Often, over 60 percent of taxes from small businesses go into the local economy (think schools, roads, parks). This is significantly higher than the taxes coming from big box stores. At Wally-World, et al, funds and taxes typically leave the local economy by going to the investors. Bees on a Bicycle, and I, by default, was developing a consciousness beyond what I'd previously considered. As a private, individual consumer, I hadn't felt a huge sense of environmental responsibility.

Now, as a retailer, my decisions affected hundreds—even thousands, considering the impact on their neighbors and family. Via social media, over a thousand people read my posts about these topics every week. I had a responsibility to share what I was learning. As an educator, I put my tools to use to inform others to make good choices in their communities. As a marketer, I created language to inform and change buying behavior. In a way, it was like the ripple effect, Chattanooga-style. For me personally, it was a good use of my "tried everything" past!

I was also learning which relationships were right for Bees. It was important to find my tribe of not only customers and vendors but also partners to help with varied efforts when the need arose. One such partner arrived and declared the space not cleaned to her specifications, furniture in the wrong place, and more—changes were needed right away! We did our best to suit her needs, and she did her work. After she finished for the day, I informed her it would be her last with us. I was looking for partners to lend a hand rather than find fault, complain, and order the team around.

Literally ten minutes after I ended that partnership, a customer approached me with a suggestion about a friend of hers who does the same thing. She hadn't heard anything in that she arrived after the disgruntled partner left. The person she recommended remains a partner of Bees to this day and is also one of our Zen Waterers.

Another time, I took a meeting with Sherri and Mary, a young set of entrepreneurs. One called me rude while the other asked me not to speak—three times. I left the meeting somewhat shaken. I had been in hundreds of meetings at my communication firm, several of which got quite heated. This one with Mary and Sherri ranked second behind an internet millionaire who had hired us to do web work for her pet project nonprofit. As she pounded on the table and shouted, her staff's faces turned all shades of red. We fired that client and didn't look back.

After we adjourned, I looked at Mary and Sherri in the parking lot, shaking their heads and talking. I could tell by their body language that they were not pleased at how I'd clearly misbehaved in their opinion. I decided to call it and walked out to them in my parking lot.

"Listen. We don't have to do this. Let's just call it a day," I said, perfectly willing to walk away from the whole deal.

"Well, Cath, what you don't realize about business is . . ." Mary explained to me. I was standing there, but not fully listening. Instead I thought of my firm in DC: the branding work we'd done for CareerBuilder.com and the contract work we did for the United States Senate. I thought about the $10,000 communication plans I'd written, the facility, operations, and payroll I managed for over a decade, and the hundreds of client negotiations I handled.

Sure, explain all you want about business to me, Mary. What I know about business is that when someone mansplains to another woman, you let them blather on like the authority they think themselves to be and let them hang.

I responded with my best, "Uh huh," and left it at that.

Happily after kissing a few toads, we settled into several really great partnerships. Many of our partners hug us and call us to ask how we are in between projects. It is a really congenial working partnership, very different from any I've had before. What I realized is the ones that didn't work before were right for others, just not for us, and that is OK.

As we rolled into our one-year anniversary, involvement from the community came in clumps, rather than through individuals. A teacher gave an assignment with extra credit for learning about the native plants available at Bees. She called first to see if that was OK. "Can my students come with their parents to see native plants and ask you questions?"

I thought for less than a second and replied, "Of course!"

Another time, a friend had gone through a divorce and moved to a smaller house. She wanted to keep her kids allowance and gardening consistent, but no longer had a garden. I had one though! She asked, "Would it be OK to have the kids come water your plants, and I'll pay them their allowance?" Uh, that was a no-brainer.

Next, the Chamber needed a 12th stop on the business crawl and scavenger hunt. Soon, 70 teams piled into Bees to search for clues. Before Christmas, a street fair on Main with 15,000 people combined efforts with Bees to have a drawing netting over 2,000 interested people watching progress on Facebook and in person. Generosity and creativity surrounded this little business.

"Can I have some more of your flyers?" a new customer asked. "I want to put them out at our coffee shop to spread the word."

A new friend added "Did you see the magazine article about you guys I put out for people to see at my party? I want everyone to go shop at Bees!" It was amazing.

I had developed many brands in the past, but this was the strongest brand I had created yet, and I was just getting started. It was weird sometimes. We attended a party or went to a restaurant and heard snippets of conversation: bees . . . bicycle . . . bees on . . . people were talking about us! Meanwhile, people came into the store and looked at me quizzically. It took me a while to put together that they were staring at someone they'd only seen online or in pictures from magazines. There I was, walking and talking. I learned to quickly crack a joke or offer plant advice to ease the way.

One day, I met with someone who had only seen me on TV. I was ankle deep in algae-infested water at the time. We had yet to get the balance of the pond right, and the fish were in a holding pot, awaiting a freshly scrubbed home. As Queen Bee (a title Graham gave me that stuck) of this little business, it was my job to do. Our intern Brennan was strategically placed down the hill. She had inexplicably volunteered to siphon off the pond water. She was always eager to learn a new skill. We on the upper part of the hill could hardly keep a straight face. Oh, the things you learn in college! One of our repeat customers was all set to give pointers for siphoning success. Soon after, there I stood, scooping out what couldn't be siphoned.

Next, I looked up to see a beautifully made-up face, not a wrinkle or blemish to be found. "Hello!" she said. "May I interview you about the recent Supreme Court decision about online sales tax?"

"Why, yes," I replied. "May I have a minute to get out of the fish pond?" A few minutes later, I was being filmed for the local nightly news.

Our one-year anniversary arrived. We had achieved much and had many miles to go. We decided to have a party to mark the day and invited our many new customers—including many who had become friends, vendors, volunteers, interns, and others who had supported the business. As we had done with our Christmas open house, Graham and I got into the kitchen and created a buffet of goodies. We set up a tent in the top of the parking

Cath helps a customer at Bees

lot and cracked open champagne. Guests arrived, bought plants, and had a great time. Then the skies got dark . . . and darker.

Bees sits about a mile from Lookout Mountain,

named after maneuvers in the Civil War. The wind whips down the side of that mountain and heads towards Market Street with a vengeance. We learned early to put pots in strategic places so they wouldn't fly around like cannonballs.

We waited as long as we could during the party to batten down the hatches. We were having a grand time, and people were cued up to buy their finds. I continued checking out customers and bagging up purchases inside. After a time, I noticed it was quieter inside the store, and people seemed distracted. I looked out to see what was going on. There was Graham with three of our customers, all of them holding onto the four legs of a 12-foot tent. To say that the metal tent and covering were bending back and forth like a wet noodle is an understatement.

After a time, Graham came inside, dripping wet. "That tent is going in the trash," he decreed. For Mr. Thrifty, that was quite a statement. The tent was so mangled, it took very little to get the pieces into the garbage bin. Oh, my. Bees was now one year old.

CHAPTER NINE:

Finding Beauty in Small

Small things can have great power.

—Cath Shaw Truelove

When you own a business, you are, as the saying goes, chief cook and bottle washer. In that role, I often find myself planting demonstration pots or beds and dealing with bugs, sun, and all else, including customers. Soon after the first anniversary, we had decided to plant two large horse troughs with plants at the entrance to Bees. I had selected no fewer than 33 plants and was digging holes in the soil Brennan and I had wheelbarrowed over from a cubic yard delivered earlier that week.

As I planted, I felt something under my hat. I rearranged my ponytail and couldn't find any evidence of what might be bothering me. I proceeded to garden.

Again, I felt something. Eeegads. Off came my hat, I tipped my head and hair over, and a more thorough search began then and there on the sidewalk. Just as I found a beetle and cheered about it a little bit, a horrified customer appeared. "Are you Cath, the owner of Bees?" she asked.

Beetle and hat firmly in hand, I respond affirmatively to the question with what was left of my dignity. Small things like beetles make big differences sometimes.

One day, I was at Bees with Pat, one of the Zen Waterers. It was raining, and we were entering data when the phone rang. "Are you going to be open until six?"

It was 5:40 and raining, but sure, we'd be there until six. "Yes, we'll be here," I replied.

"Good! I'll be right over!" Ten minutes later, Alicia bounced through the door. "This is my happy place, and I want stuff from here at my wedding. Let's go look at what you have," she said. We gathered our umbrellas and out we went to see what made sense for her.

"We bought a house. It's a fixer-upper and needs a garden. I want things from Bees in the garden, but let's use them in the wedding first."

What? We weren't a florist and didn't do wedding bouquets.

"We can plant these plants and have them as center-pieces," Alicia said.

I was still catching up mentally from entering data a few minutes before and looked at her blankly. We stood there in the lot among the plants with our umbrellas, rain dripping off the side of each. She then grabbed my arm and looked me in the eye. "You can do this! I want Bees to do this!"

I eventually got with the program and came up with a plan: we'd plant around 60 herbs and small perennials in grain-fiber pots and mulch them, just like little mini-gardens. After the wedding, I'd work with her and her new husband Chris to arrange them in their garden. I asked when her wedding was. "In two weeks," she replied. In the world of weddings and events, that is the equivalent of ten minutes from now. We also wanted the plants to grow a bit to fill out the containers. We'd be planting them the very next day.

Fourteen days later, the centerpieces had grown in and looked lovely. I had visions of the happy couple planting the contents in their new garden after the wedding. The whole project was beyond idyllic and fit perfectly into our environmental approach. The day of the wedding, we were also holding a workshop on dyeing with indigo at the store. Participants were happily dyeing and chatting outside.

I watered the plants one last time to give them a boost before packing them for transport. Oops! Water everywhere. No problem, I'll just scoot this table closer to the drain in the floor. Bam! One side of the table collapsed, and all 13 centerpieces crashed to the floor two hours before the wedding. Members of the indigo-dyeing class rushed in to see what the clatter was. I stood there in shock, trying not to cry. Graham rushed in and soothed me. Mercifully, only one container had broken. The remaining ones were Auburn University Orange, and I knew Alicia's family would not permit that. This family took football seriously, and the container colors had been selected accordingly.

Graham and I grabbed the Hammered Bronze spray paint I use for most any fix-it project and prayed for the best. We had two hours to get that paint dry on the replacement pot to take the place of the broken one. We also needed to re-mulch everything and wash off the plants that had dirt dumped on them. In record time, I left to install the centerpieces. I don't know how, but the spray-painted one matched the others perfectly. Neither Graham nor I could keep track of which one was the hidden Auburn Orange container.

Besides our snafu, I was doubly nervous because of the venue. I had secretly hoped the wedding would be at a low-key place in case my first try looked horrible. Nope. It was at the Turnbull Building, number nine in the world's top ten venues for 2018 according to *Venue Magazine*. Great. No pressure there.

As I exited, I ran into Chris, the groom. "What a shit show this all is," he said gleefully. I opened and shut my mouth, wisely saving my own shit show story for later. If he only knew. Here I was, putting centerpieces together for this beautiful couple in one of the most sought after venues in the world—with a staff of one plus maybe one volunteer if I got lucky. Florists around town routinely had team pictures with six, eight, and sometimes ten staff members. Bees may have been small, but it was effective, even when the entire project took a tumble!

When I returned to Bees after the installation, Graham met me outside in the plant area and dipped me for a passionate kiss. He was proud of me. Other people noticed too; cars driving by hooted their horns and people cheered in approval of our public display of affection. Though Graham was the one doing the kissing, I really fell in love with Chattanooga in that moment. What camaraderie from passerby!

Inside Bees on a Bicycle

As I walked back inside to take on the next task, I thought about another time when being small had great impact. In a previous role to mine at Bees, I organized the volunteers, funding, and communication for four, 24-hour marathons benefiting 83 small, struggling nonprofits. When we stayed up all night working to produce communications for these groups, we often marveled at how much they could do with a very small staff and budget. In turn, with a small team, we could assist so many, and the organizations, in turn supported thousands of people. Countless times, I have thought of the mark these small nonprofits made on society. They moved mountains, as Mom would say.

Bees is located on two-tenths of an acre and decidedly smaller than other garden centers. We must be creative about what we provide so people won't be frustrated by our offerings. We knew people were checking us out; one even showed up with a clipboard. When asked, she replied "They asked me to photograph each section and write prices down." Sometimes visitors from other retailers ask us questions. I've learned to train the interns for such occasions because they rarely press me, the face of the business, for information. On such occasions, when asked about competitors, we share our philosophy of abundance: "There's room at the table for all of us." And we leave it at that.

We, too, wanted to know what similar retailers were doing. To me, competitor research is more about differentiation than figuring out what they are up to and how to duplicate it. One summer, we visited a large urban garden center in another city. At their large, two-acre site, we looked at their perennials. They had more of them, but we had a wider assortment. We looked at their pots. Again, they had more, but we had a wider assortment. After that field trip, we didn't feel so badly about the options we displayed. In addition, many customers are delighted by our smallness and appreciate our boutique, friendly, and educational approach.

Our small footprint forces me to take stock of the little things and appreciate them. Rather than focusing outward on what similar companies are doing, we focus inward on what we are accomplishing anew and how best to do it well. As a result, I've developed habits about getting work done mindfully and purposefully. I take time for conversations with interns, customers, and Zen Waterers. I drink tea and savor quiet moments in ways I never did before. I appreciate bees and wasps getting a drink of water in a saucer we laid out in the sun. I marvel at how an intern can water all 18 plants in a flat with care.

Cath with a broken ankle, gardening at the big house

Sometimes though, it was sheer determination. Years before Bees, I had broken my ankle in three places, dislocating my foot. It took six months to learn to walk again. Despite being on crutches and walking with a cane for half a year, I gardened. Determination was not new to me.

During our first year, though we were experiencing many-fold growth with new customers finding us daily, many people didn't know we existed. It takes time with any small business to make a mark. I continued to develop my patience, and monitored any negative self-talk on quiet days. I also used this time to sit and think and imagine. This led to a stream, of sorts, to forge to fund new initiatives.

As the second year approached, it became clear we needed money to fund next steps. The company had been funded until this point by savings and the court case from Mom's death. I didn't want to incur debt, so it was time to get creative and deal with the last of the estates. For years, I hadn't been able to bring myself to sort out what sat, untouched, in a grocery bag inside a security box. It was time to process it, both in my mind and my heart, and for Bees to grow.

Mom was one of those people who bought jewelry rather than spending money on shoes, sports equipment, or going to the movies. If life were simpler, that last portion of Mom's estate would have been one big item like a cabin in the woods. But no, Mom bought jewelry. Not one big thing, but lots of little things. Now, if you do research, you will find that cars and jewelry are the very worst places to put money if you want return. Thus, her jewelry stayed in a bag in a safety deposit box for years. Her rings and bracelets were exquisite. But good taste aside, this needed sorting through for a pathway to next steps with the business. Recently, a friend noted the wisdom in the timing of this: the jewelry had been just enough trouble to stay in that form for an investment at the right time.

Graham did some research and found a great independent appraiser. I went to get the bag out of the safety deposit box. Included were two diamonds Graham had found at the bottom of another safety deposit box we rented in Virginia (Yes, we found diamonds!), along with a host of Mom's treasures. Memories of when I'd melted down odd earrings after my divorce for grocery money came into my head. I couldn't believe I was doing this again.

Selling jewelry is definitely a first-world problem to solve. I realize many folks struggle to put food on the table, and I came very close to that after my divorce just years before. My go-to jewelry is a set of silver earrings from Target. I am not a big jewelry person, yet stored Mom's treasures for years for sentimental reasons.

A day later, I piled my loot, still in the grocery bag, and a small suitcase into my car and drove to Nashville. I had an afternoon appointment with the independent appraiser Graham had found. She would advise me at an hourly rate. She also had gold and gem connections that could come in handy, depending on what was worth selling. She set to work making small piles of 9, 14, 18 and 22-carat gold. I looked at two bracelets my dad and I had bought in Abu Dhabi and took a deep breath. She handed me tissues. This was an emotional process. "These are all the right things, just in the wrong places," she said. It was an amazing way of allowing me to let go and let this just be a process, not an emotional journey.

Still, I thought about those bracelets. Not only was I letting go of Mom's pretty things, but also memories with my Dad and our travels together in foreign lands. I told the appraiser how we bought those bracelets in a glorified flea market in the late 1970s. They were displayed on a wooden dowel behind a wobbly sheet of plexiglass at night. One could easily kick it in and take an armload of gold, but no thievery was present in Abu Dhabi in those days, I suppose. What a different land.

Dad and I selected two bangles from the hundreds displayed, and I wore them that summer with pride. Little housing was available in Abu Dhabi back then, and we lived in a hotel, along with many other engineers and their families brought in to make Abu Dhabi what we know it as today. I made friends quickly that summer. The Fleetwood Mac album *Rumors* was the favorite of my friend Ashraf, who would drive his limo (those were the cars available there at that time) with a gang of us from one end of Abu Dhabi and back again. We'd drink rum and Cokes and sing "'The Chain" as loudly as we could, then clamber into the Hilton Disco to dance all night, returning to the hotel where we all lived around 3 am. I was 14. When I returned to the States for 9th grade, people asked me, "What did you do last summer? Did you go to camp?" Yeah, I went to . . . camp.

I got quiet after sharing that story and let the appraiser

finish her work. Later, she asked me to dinner, and I was all storied out. That day I vividly experienced that jewelry has memories and energy in it—at least, I think so. I was an exhausted and quiet dinner guest that evening.

The next day, I met with the gem guy. One ring had a stone in it that could be of value. He also wanted to assess two other items. The meeting was one of the most bizarre I've ever attended. The diamond merchant was Israeli, and his father still lived in Israel. He'd ask, "May I video this?" and upon my permission, he'd turn the piece of jewelry this way and that in front of his phone. A moment later, he'd be in earnest conversation in Arabic with his dad in Israel. He'd shout a number to me, and I'd either nod in agreement or say no. This went on for two hours.

After that, I sat in the lobby and collected my thoughts. I'd agreed to melt down gold, sold a diamond, and assessed the value of a set of treasured objects—all in less than 24 hours. All my mom's pretty things were gone. Dad's and mine too. My bracelets from Abu Dhabi were to be melted down and sold for scrap. I was ashamed and also freed. It was confusing. All those dead people, old memories like anniversaries, birthdays, and more, flooded me. I had melted it down and sold it away.

As said by the appraiser the previous day, "These are all the right things, just in the wrong place." Those words rang true. They allowed me to take the next steps I wanted to at Bees and to live in the present.

While there in the lobby, I thought about other small and powerful things. Our garden center was small but growing in its role in our community as well as wider audiences online. I was constantly awed at how my words and educational online posts affected people as far away as Australia. As I made environmentally-savvy buying choices and shared my beliefs, I heard about people who, in turn, changed their buying habits. Small but significant; it held power for me.

I considered the concept of doing more with less and how that worked for Bees at the time. We were doing a massive social media, YouTube and PR strategy, writing this book, managing eight events, and running the shop with a staff of one plus occasional volunteer and intern assistance. When it came to human resources, this was definitely less with more!

Indeed that day in the lobby, I had my share of deep thoughts. I continued thinking. I quietly celebrated how this was the last of an office, house with my ex, and five estates (Dad, Mom, Graham's Mom, and Dad's two parents) of stuff I had touched and sorted. It was the end of a long journey. I walked out of the lobby with my purse and an empty grocery bag and drove back to Chattanooga. The right place for all Mom's and Dad's treasures that day was not with me. It took me years to admit that I had different goals than they did when it came to beautiful jewelry.

As I drove back to Chattanooga, I thought of my mom. I missed her desperately and wished she were with me on this journey of building a business. She would have adored Bees on a Bicycle. I remembered her small set of gold earrings from India that I had sold. She probably purchased them on one of her trips to town. Dad and she lived in a remote part of India in the 1960s during one

Mom a few years before moving to India

of Dad's engineering projects. Engineers and their wives often wanted items from the city. Mom would add all the items to her shopping list, then travel into the city alone by train. All the other wives either weren't allowed or were too scared to travel alone in those days. Not Mom! She'd go by train, then spend the night in the city, returning the next day. She had a movie-star quality to her appearance and must have been quite a vision.

I weighed the concept of small things versus the concept of doing more with less. How did this work for me in that moment? The most obvious was that, now that there was capital to add to what the business was making, we could leapfrog forward to what was next. We considered ecommerce, plant rentals, and getting into the wedding market. One clear possibility was adding the capability to sell indoor plants. But this was complicated by the pervasive use of chemicals in indoor plant propagation. This, and the need to winter-over unsold stock, required shelter and sufficient light beyond the facility we had. We began shopping for greenhouses and planning. For a business that wanted to focus on simple, small things, it was getting complicated fast.

As we moved forward, I thought a lot about stuff. I had spent years sorting and selling estate items. Now I was amassing stuff for others to buy. One day, a customer spent the better part of an hour looking carefully at each item for sale. "You're a minimalist!" she concluded, and she was correct. I respect beautiful things, but not lots of them. I aim to help people marry what they treasure with new and cherished objects from Bees. Hopefully, several of these will be environmentally sustainable as well. If someone has read *The Life-changing Magic of Tidying Up* by Marie Kondo, they've found a home and a sympathetic ear at Bees. We aren't about amassing much, but rather narrowing down to fabulousness, fun, and delight.

The years leading to Bees were one big exercise in tidying up. I moved to a new city and started over with the love of my life at my side. He eventually married me too. With his help, I've created a business with heart and a conscience. It has a long way to go, but it is beloved by many already. So much so by several that they volunteer their time to be a part of it.

There is a need for heart-based businesses, and Bees on a Bicycle definitely fits into that category. There is a role for community-based entities like ours that make a difference. The lines between nonprofits and businesses of this kind are blurring as doing good while providing products and services merge. Large companies nod their heads toward a heart-centered approach with corporate training, but it is my belief that smaller companies are better positioned for an authentic, heart-centered approach. Why? They are closer to the ground, where the customers are struggling. The leadership is present to listen. They are nimble and quick to respond. Big companies are like big ships that take much longer to turn around, despite their corporate social responsibility efforts.

A good example of this idea within garden centers is what I call the wounded gardener. Time after time, folks came to Bees just short of tears. They had killed plant after plant and broken container after container. Alternatively, they had fallen for a bright, blingy plant filled with chemicals and upon bringing it home, interrupted its supply of the equivalent of plant steroids. What these customers didn't know is that they fell into a planned obsolescence trap of annuals that die after a season and poorly made, non-winterized pots. They blamed themselves, but were not at fault. We answer their queries and soothe their fears. As a result, we prepare many educational social media posts, blog articles, workshops, newsletters, speeches, and community-based appearances. It is our hope that gardening will become a healing practice for more people as a result.

As business owners, we often equate success with growth and growth with big things. What I have learned from Bees is that small is beautiful. It allows us to talk to customers. It allows me to have great relationships with vendors, potential employees, customers who grow into friends, interns, my husband, and myself. Bigger isn't better when it comes to Bees. We enjoy the simple things as the community surrounds us. I may not have my Shaw family, but the Truelove family now has me as a member, and the Chattanooga community has welcomed me into their midst. I am no longer lost.

In a weird way, my new clogs represent how I've found life here. I'd worn my old ones one too many times to walk the dog, and the sole finally split open, allowing water to enter. I love my new clogs. They are the exact same kind as before, just newer and whole. They fit in a way that makes me want to stand up straighter. I am thankful for my new shoes.

Years ago, I drove a BMW, wore clothes from Nordstrom, and networked over ridiculously overpriced breakfasts with other .com internet folks. How things have changed. These days, I am thankful for my new shoes, the life I have here in Chattanooga, a husband who loves me, and our sweet dog Fred. After work, I dance in the kitchen and share a glass of wine with my loved one as Fred watches. I am thankful for these fine moments, however simple. Let the small moments of life take one step at a time into my heart. Let the peace I find there be a part of what people find at Bees. I'm thankful.

I am grateful for a set of customers who are willing to grow and learn as Bees grows. This next year, we will implement a seasonal marketing, event, merchandise, and goal-setting schedule. Beginning with the start of winter on December 21, hibernation and recharging (just like perennial plants!) will be implemented. Gone is the 12-month-a-year grind, and something more refined and natural will be put in its place. Being available only by appointment for two months isn't typical retail, but it is typical garden. We here at Bees—and, in turn, our customers—will embrace how we live here in one big garden: Earth.

CALLIE CANTRELL

Bees on a Bicycle as seen from Market Street.

One of my favorite cartoon characters is Mighty Mouse. His tiny but mighty ways inspire me. There is so much that can be done in tiny doses, in small environments. When it comes to restoring our pollinator populations, this tiny but mighty approach is essential—in many states, 98 percent of the land is privately owned! I began thinking about how a small garden center could make a difference. One advantage is that being small allows us to turn on a dime and respond to environmental as well as customer needs and trends. In addition, it allows us to fill a niche.

Bees is based in Chattanooga, though our reach online is international. Customers generally come from within 30 miles, but we have a growing set of travelers from Atlanta, Nashville, and other locales that make us part of their Chattanooga itinerary. One day we may have ecommerce, but not right now. Chattanooga, though with its liberal facets, is nestled at the base of Tennessee, a largely politically conservative state. Communicating what I've learned about monarch butterfly decline, alternatives to plastic, and pollinator-friendly native plants, among other related topics, has sometimes been a bit of an uphill climb among those who thought the environment was fine as is. Mighty Mouse remains as my hero as we find a way.

CONCLUSION:

What's Next?

As we went to press, six new, large apartment buildings are almost done with construction within half a mile of Bees, ripe for balcony gardens and walking distance from urban garden adventures. Two blocks of townhouses are halfway done, just a short walk away. The largest house to date in Chattanooga's Historic Southside District (they've rebranded since Bees began) was underway across 19th street, just steps away from Bees on a Bicycle's main entrance. The vacant lot next door was slated to begin construction upon the house's completion. The boarded-up buildings across Market Street remained.

As Bees grows, my role in the community solidifies. I'm recognized at events and have lost my anonymous, invisible status. Business systems and traditions are sliding into place. Income is realized. Friendships and business relationships have and are forming. Through this book and a resulting speaking tour, I began to reach out beyond Chattanooga and am sharing my story to inspire groups: young women and men about to embark on careers, those of us going through similar change and transition, and all of us finding our way. In addition, key messages about the environment, the plight of pollinators, and related topics continue to be discussed. I am giving workshops and have started a video series on YouTube, as well as appearances on local television. My garden chats and home talks use gardening as a metaphor for organizing special places in the home and along our path in life.

In Gratitude

In a perfect bit of timing, I write this as Graham pre-
pares fruitcake for Thanksgiving with friends this week.
The scents of dried fruits, cinnamon, and nuts fill our
home. Henry is on his way from Atlanta. We plan to visit
Carol, Graham's sister, and her family in a few weeks. I
am thankful for this new family that shared their lovely
last name with me. No longer am I alone as the last Shaw,
but rather the newest Truelove until a newborn or another
bride joins our ranks.

Each day I am ever grateful for the six incredible
women that stand with me as dear friends. I hope to know
and love Jayne, Marcia, Gigi, Lise, Michelle, and Michele
for all my remaining days. As I wrote this book, they were
there for me by reminding me of stories to include, what
to keep private, and how to take time to let the story flow.
They listened as I moaned about how on Earth I'd fit days
of writing in with all that we do at Bees, yet I found the
time because of my love for writing. Most of all, I'm so
pleased and thankful that they share the ups and downs

with me, every step of the way, however boring, long-winded, or repetitive I may be.

Other key friends have been there for me with tokens of kindness throughout this process. Their enthusiasm via social media, spreading the word, notes in the mail, and texts bolsters me and brightens my day. Thank you, Catherine, Gracie, Julie, Dawn and Derek, Susan Ann, Theresa, Linda, Susan, Annie, and Sara.

I am thankful for my mom and all she taught me about living life fully. Her vitality gave me my passion and tenacity. Her tragic passing and resulting court case, though bittersweet, allowed me to start Bees. It sounds odd to be thankful for this, but without this sequence of events years before, I'd not be able to choose this path. There is not a day that passes without my wishing she were here among us to see her legacy and share it with us. Her spirit and memory support me. From Mom, I've learned I can move mountains!

For my new Chattanooga friends, I am indebted for their generosity and spirit. Not a week goes by without someone reaching out to see how they can connect with and support our little shop. It is such a blessing to be in such a great community. I especially recognize Mary Lou, Betsy, Cris, Adrienne, Cherita, Steph, Keith and Danny, Jennifer and Grant and their sons Aaron and Jake, Tobi and David and their son Eli, Jaimie, Beth, Nikki, Barb, Shelli, and the Chattanooga Chamber of Commerce ambassadors, notably Kay, Dan, Marie, and Haley.

My team at Un-Settling Books has played a vital role in the development of this book as well as for me personally. Their approach to book writing is refreshing and unique. To be included in the group of writers you support is such an honor. Many thanks to Maggie as well as Sky.

Designers Karen Culp Lili Picou have been on hand to creatively steer Bees into graphic design beauty and I am forever grateful. Thanks also to Matt Lively, the artist of the mural that inspired Bees on a Bicycle's name, who generously worked with us to provide cover art that really sang for this book.

Vendors, assorted Chattanooga City officials, and key clients have also formed close bonds with us at Bees, and I am forever grateful for their keen ideas, encouragement, and kind gestures. Thank you, Dennis, Paul, John, Emily, Michael, Missy, Ty, Scott, Teresa, Rebecca, Sarah, Alicia, and Chris.

Our first set of interns will always be close to my heart. I cherish and thank Bryanna, Madison, Mary Stuart, and Brennan, who is like a daughter to me. May they be joined by many other interns who welcome on-site learning of entrepreneurial pursuits, small business success, and more. I taught Brennan how to bake a potato and do taxes—the list of what can be learned at Bees is endless!

The Chattanooga garden community has been a boundless source of wisdom, encouragement and support. Thank you, Ann, Nora, Kristina, Missy, Phyllis, Susan, and many others from an ever-growing set of garden clubs embracing Bees and our work.

Thanks go to the Zen Waterers and all that they do.

At the time of this publication, Mary Lou, Pat, Lindsey, Katie, Marcelle, Steph, and Graham join us at Bees to help as the need arises. The list grows as we morph and change. We are blessed by their sense of community and support of small, local business. Being at a garden shop is good for the soul, and they make use of that knowledge by spending time with us.

I am truly thankful for Henry and Julia for accepting me as the person who stands by their dad. I burst into their world quickly, and in good time, they welcomed me into their hearts. I am grateful that they have shared their beloved dad with me.

Not that he is much of a reader and will see this, but I want to acknowledge Fred's role in my life and my thankfulness for his doggy heart. He is truly a healing and generous soul. I am so lucky to have him as part of my home and frequent companion as I run Bees.

Last and most importantly, I am thankful for Graham. I could not have come to this point, written this book, or run Bees on a Bicycle without his many talents. He fixes things, cooks, offers encouraging words, and is there to love me, however crabby and disappointed I may be. He is an incredible mate, and I am so glad he chose me to be his wife and partner in life forever.

About the Author

Cath Shaw Truelove

Cath owns Bees on a Bicycle, a garden center and gift shop located on Market Street in the heart of Chattanooga, Tennessee's vibrant Southside community. Ms. Truelove, who has farming roots from both sides of her family, formerly owned a DC-based landscaping business called Garden of Urban. As part of her work, she developed an inner-city science and math program introducing over 400 youth to gardening. She was certified as a Master Gardener years ago and is known for her gardens featuring both native and exotic plants.

Cath is a recognized speaker and writer who built a viable communications agency from the ground up, employing 54 people over 12 years with clients ranging from the US Senate to CareerBuilder.com. Previous to that, she coordinated nationwide efforts to recruit, train, schedule, and acknowledge 700 volunteers for the AIDS Memorial Quilt. In another speaking tour, she led efforts nationwide within the interior design industry to increase capacity by 1,000 new beds in homeless shelters.

Cath recently married Graham Truelove and got the best last name a girl could ask for. She lives in the Northshore Chattanooga with Graham and her dog, Fred.

Join the Bees Community!

Continued conversations

We are considering a set of online chats, workbooks, and an inspirational deck of cards for entrepreneurs who are dreaming of tiny but mighty ventures like Bees on a Bicycle. If you are interested in learning more about this, join our mailing list at www.beesonabicycle.com, and you will be the first to learn about upcoming sessions.

A special gift for our readers

When you are in Chattanooga, stop by the shop, show your book or an email from one of the lists below, and receive a 40 percent discount on one item less than $150.00! You will want to check out our hours online first, in that we aren't open all the time! We are located at 1909 Market Street, Chattanooga, TN 37408. Parking is available in our lot, on Emerson Street adjacent to the property, and at the end of the block at Cornerstone Church at 19th and Long Streets. Hours and a map of our location can be found online at www.beesonabicycle.com. See you soon!

Staying in touch

- Hear about book readings, book-related events, future books, or other related publications, at www.beesonabicycle.com/book

- Inquire about Cath speaking to your organization visit at www.beesonabicycle.com/contact

- View Cath's videos on gardening and décor at www.youtube.com (search for Bees on a Bicycle)

- Subscribe to the Bees on a Bicycle blog at www.beesonabicycle.com/journal-in-your-inbox

- Join the Bees on a Bicycle mailing list at www.beesonabicycle.com. A form for our mailing list is on our home page.

Readers' Guide

The following activities and questions are intended to enrich your reading experience. Both individuals and small groups or book clubs can pick and choose to fit their needs. Have fun with this! The less serious you can be, the more you will get out of it!

Activities

1. Send one of the questions below to select members of your group to present to the others.

2. Create a collage illustrating one of the chapters, with the various emotions and challenges Cath faced and your interpretation of them. The pictures don't need to be literal. For example, a red wall could represent frustration or anger.

3. Get a piece of butcher paper or poster board. Draw circles representing various communities in your life, for example family, church, work,

neighborhood, friends, and so on. Draw over-
lapping circles where someone may be in several such communities, for example, your wife
or husband. Please note: this activity can take
hours and is best done individually. It is very
telling and can bring out all sorts of observa-
tions about your world. For extra credit, put a
star or otherwise highlight someone of particular significance to you in each community.

4.   Have the members of your group stand up. Pose
solutions to one of the topics in the questions below
and assign parts of the room to each. Have the
members choose their response by walking to the
part of the room that signifies their choice. For
example, if the question is, "What is your favorite animal?" then a possibility is that all the dog
lovers would stand by the door, the cat people
would be by the sofa, and the turtle folks would be
by the bookcase. To expand the conversation, have
one or two expand upon their choice and share
their thoughts with the group. Repeat 4-5 times.

5.   Write the following topics on separate slips of
paper for people in your group to draw individually or in groups of two. After reading their
selection to the group, share your interpretation or
what you remember on this topic from reading the
book. Alternate format: Break into small groups
of 2-3 members. Assign one of the topics listed
below to each small group. Allow 3–5 minutes to

discuss. Then each group shares their assigned
topic and their thoughts and interpretations.

a. The love of a dog is loyal and kind
b. Journeys of the soul are rarely travelled in
    straight lines
c. Some careers are more logical than others
d. Doing more with less
e. Finding beauty in the small things
f. Community comes when you are ready
g. Clearing within vs clearing your space
h. Finding what you cherish among what you
    have responsibility for
i. Sorting stuff and what to do
j. Losing someone suddenly vs losing
    someone from a long illness
k. Opinions of others and my response
l. Driving a BMW vs riding the bus
m. Appropriate timing for dating after divorce
n. Entrepreneurialism vs working for
    companies.

Questions

1. When Cath was left by her dad and lived
    with the woman he was divorcing, what
    would you have done in her shoes?

2. Of the various jobs Cath had in her life, which
    one would you like to try for a week or two?

3. Cath identifies six women to stand by her side

and one husband. Who are the folks of similar stature in your life? Do you feel obligated to have family members fill each of these spots or at least some of them? Why or why not?

4. Cath inherited approximately 100 scarves. Have you inherited something like this with sentimental value but of no use (too many to use in this case). How would you handle this situation, knowing that you cherished each of them?

5. At the time of the book, what's Cath's way of asking God (or whatever you may call your higher power or Universe) for what she wants? Is she friendly or spooked about receiving things out of her control at Bees? What is your way to ask the universe for what you want? Have you received anything recently that was an uncanny coincidence you can't explain? Do you see this as just weird timing or the universe answering your thoughts?

6. How have you experienced being and feeling being a small part of a big universe? Where in the book does Cath experience this?

7. How reliant are you on your GPS? If you lost signal in the woods like Cath did, what would be your next steps?

8. Cath inherited eight junker cars. What would you have done?

9. What news from a family member or friend

shocked you to the core? What did you do?
What news did Cath receive like this?

10. How many houses in Cath's and Graham's old neighborhood can you name?

11. When have you been sure about the future?
When in the book (hint: driving over a bridge)
does Cath predict the future? What other
intuitions does Cath have in the book?

12. How many places in the book, before
Chattanooga, did Cath live in?

13. Cath tried many times to find work. Have you
or someone else you know struggled with finding employment? What strategies were used?

14. Imagine travelling to the Middle East
alone at age 14. Would you send your
kid today to do that? How would you
have felt at that age on that voyage?

15. Do you ever dream of owning your own
business? What would it look like? What
is stopping you from taking this path?

Made in the USA
Columbia, SC
16 December 2022

74183208R00104